NAPOLEON'S
EVERYDAY
GOURMET
GRILLING

Perfect Rack of Lamb, page 212

GOURMET GRILLS

NAPOLEON'S
EVERYDAY
GOURMET
GRILLING

INSPIRED RECIPES
BY CHEF **TED READER**

KEY PORTER BOOKS

To all those who love to grill and barbecue.
From the beginner to the pro, make your belly a
delicious, happy place.

—CHEF TED READER

The inspiration for our first hardcover cookbook
comes from a passionate love of grilling and our
appreciation of proud Napoleon owners over the
past many years. This book and the hard work
put into it is dedicated to them and everyone at
Napoleon Appliance Corporation who have been
crafting and building our gourmet grills to ensure
our customers' total satisfaction and share our
true passion of grilling.

—NAPOLEON APPLIANCE CORPORATION

Library and Archives Canada Cataloguing in Publication

Reader, Ted
    Napoleon's everyday gourmet grilling / by Ted Reader.

Includes index.
ISBN 978-1-55470-151-3

    1. Barbecue cookery. I. Napoleon Appliance Corporation
II. Title. III. Title: Everyday gourmet grilling.
TX840.B3R4245 2009   641.5'784   C2008-906989-7

ONTARIO ARTS COUNCIL
CONSEIL DES ARTS DE L'ONTARIO

The publisher gratefully acknowledges the support of the Canada Council for the Arts and the Ontario Arts Council for its publishing program. We acknowledge the support of the Government of Ontario through the Ontario Media Development Corporation's Ontario Book Initiative.

We acknowledge the financial support of the Government of Canada through the Book Publishing Industry Development Program (BPIDP) for our publishing activities.

Key Porter Books Limited
Six Adelaide Street East, Tenth Floor
Toronto, Ontario
Canada M5C 1H6

www.keyporter.com

Design: Martin Gould
Photography: Mike McColl (except page 202, photo courtesy of Napoleon®)

Printed and bound in Canada

09 10 11 12 13 6 5 4 3 2 1

As the largest family owned hearth and grill manufacturer in North America, Napoleon maintains strong family values that carry through in every aspect of the organization. Since 1976, Napoleon has grown from a small manufacturing operation to a large private corporation instilling the same solid values it began with. Napoleon products are found in homes around the globe and have become the preferred brand choice worldwide.

TABLE OF CONTENTS

Grilled Chocolate Lobster Tails, page 282

FOREWORD

A warm welcome to all you grilling enthusiasts!

Today we use the term "barbecue" rather widely to describe any type of food prepared on a grill by various methods. But in reality it involves much more than food preparation. It's a philosophy and a lifestyle.

What could be more ideal than gathering with family and friends to share in a sumptuous feast prepared on your very own grill — all in the casual, relaxed atmosphere of your backyard? Around the world, the ease and convenience of cooking on a grill has turned this way to cook into one of the most popular ways to entertain.

Cooking outdoors makes cleanup easy, and during the summer season, outdoor cooking keeps your kitchen cool. And the concept of an outdoor kitchen isn't such a new thing. A summer kitchen has been a standard item on farms for years, while in southern climates, the only practical way to cook meals is outside.

Grilling has come a long way from the days when the menu was limited to the items traditionally associated with the barbecue: hot dogs, sausages, burgers, chicken, and steak. Thanks to today's superior cooking systems, there are no limits to the type of food you can cook on a grill. From tender fish dishes to a slow rotisserie-cooked leg of lamb, from preparing a pizza to smoking some meat, from cooking on wood planks to preparing your breakfast, the unmistakable taste of food prepared on a grill is synonymous with outdoor living.

Napoleon® has partnered with Chef Ted Reader to bring you delicious and creative recipes that will excite your taste buds — and those of your guests. Whether you're throwing a last-minute party, an informal gathering, a casual meal, a holiday feast, or a family reunion, Ted Reader's passion for grilling delivers results with terrific recipes that will take you and your guests on mouth-watering food adventures.

So don't be shy. Whether you have been grilling for years or you're just starting out, you can serve up culinary delights every time. This book is jam-packed with fresh and exciting ideas for your backyard cooking. There is a recipe for every occasion, from impromptu dinners to sophisticated events. Explore and experience dishes like Grilled T-Bone Steak with Whipped Horseradish Cream, Bacon-Wrapped Scallops, Grilled Portobello Mushroom Stacks, and Roast Leg of Lamb with Rosemary, Garlic, and Lemon. Try Grilled Lobster Thermidor with Crab and Brie Crust, or cook up a storm using South Carolina Yellow Mustard Barbecue Sauce. By definition, backyard barbecues translate into a relaxed atmosphere — creating positive and lasting memories.

Now go ahead — start flipping through this exciting volume of unique culinary ideas, and become inspired by the recipes and photos you find in these pages. Choose a dish or two and start grilling like a pro. You're sure to become a backyard hero, impressing your family and friends with your cooking prowess.

–INGRID AND WOLFGANG SCHROETER

IN THE BEGINNING
CHEF TED READER

Ten years ago while working for Loblaws we developed a President's Choice Grill with Napoleon® Grills. I was lucky enough to meet Ingrid and Wolfgang and then to have them sponsor my television show King of the Q. A relationship was born that endures to this very day. I am proud to call them my friends and I am proud to say there is no grill I like to work with more. Believe me when I tell you this. There are over 17 Napoleon® grills in my back yard, or bolted to my truck, or attached to my custom smoker. They do it all for me.

Ingrid and Wolfgang Schroeter own and operate Napoleon® Grills and Fireplaces. They are two driven, passionate, and innovative people, dedicated to developing and creating the best grills in the world. They, like all perfectionists, are always focused on the prize. They have built a company based on family values that includes sons Chris and Stephen and operates manufacturing and distribution facilities in Canada, the U.S., and China. This industrious family continues to develop award-winning grills and fireplaces. In "Ted Speak," they are grills designed for the ultimate in "grilling, glazing, dipping, and licking."

I am never quite satisfied with what I do. I always know I could have done it better, farther, bigger, or more. That's why Napoleon® and I work so well together. I've taught at their BBQ University and been to the Hearth, Patio, and Barbecue Association Trade Show for them four years in a row. They are founders and sponsors of the Canadian Barbecue Association and I look forward to the Napoleon® Stage at the Great Canadian Beer Festival every year. They give my books space on their website and I give them space on my site. When the idea for this book came along it didn't require a second thought to accept the challenge.

Napoleon® has helped make me look good for years and I try to do the same for them wherever I go. I think of my big smoker rig with three Napoleon® P450 grills attached. That rig has travelled hundreds of miles to functions in both Canada and the U.S. I have beaten these grills up. Imagine thirty Beer Can Chickens packed into those grills, on that rig, in the middle of a field in Michigan. Four days later it's Pulled Pork on the ninth hole of a gold course in Stouffville, Ontario. I work my Napoleons hard and they keep on delivering delicious food to happy bellies.

Napoleon's various models fire up to 650ºF/340ºC with propane and natural gas. Their superior burners deliver strong steady heat from a superior fire box. If you're going to aim at true "low and slow" BBQ fare these are the grills that hold the heat and keep the moisture and flavours where they belong. These qualities alone have served me well — but there's more. As far as I know, these are the only gas grills that allow you to cook with charcoal at temperatures up to 750ºF/400ºC, giving you access to the great results of natural flame as well.

Now we can add the Napoleon® SIZZLE ZONE™ — infrared burners. They reach a temperature of 1800ºF/980ºC in 25 seconds flat. This is heat unaffected by wind, rain, or cold. That is perfect for fast, hot searing. That seals in moisture and flavour. That will cook you the best steak you ever ate in five minutes. That is second to none with the Napoleon® Rotisserie spinning a perfect prime rib.

We live in a world where toys matter. Someone like me who can never quite be satisfied just grilling a plain old steak needs toys. I know chefs drive people nuts sometimes with the baskets, and griddles, and planks, and needles, and on and on. Napoleon® has the toys covered too. Finding the crazy tools I come up with is no harder than visiting your local Napoleon® dealer or the Napoleon® website. If they don't have it, it's probably something I just dreamed up and they're working on it.

This book is meant to provide you with options. You can buy a really awesome Napoleon® grill with the excellent side burner and the SIZZLE ZONE™ burners for added pizzazz. You can put it in your backyard and three or four times a month you can whip up a few burgers or a steak or two. Or you can have a good look at the possibilities I offer you here and really fly. Try a prime rib. Bake some brownies. Go ahead, invite twenty friends over and throw a grill-style cocktail party. Before you know it you'll be creating your own recipes.

Napoleon® makes it easy to make it tasty and delicious. This is my opportunity to thank Ingrid and Wolfgang for all that they have done and do for me and for barbecue. It's also my opportunity to remind a few more people that cooking in general and barbecuing specifically doesn't just feed the belly — though that's definitely important. It feeds the soul. Relaxing over a meal used to be a daily thing. Now we do it only now and again. Sharing Grilled Flank Steak with Thai Marinade with a few friends is a lot cheaper than the airfare to Thailand. With a little planning and a Napoleon® in the backyard you can take a vacation from the hurly-burly any time you want.

Thanks Ingrid and thanks Wolfgang. Here's to lots more Napoleon® delicious days.

BEFORE YOU START

Barbecuing involves high heat and fire. The margin for error is small. Use the barbecue only when you will be able to give it your full attention. If you are going to be the Grill Master on a given day we suggest waiting until the grill is cooling down before you really let loose and join the party. Everybody loves to party with the grill, particularly if you just spent next month's mortgage on porterhouse steaks. It would really be a shame to destroy them now.

Your Napoleon® grill zone is your kingdom. Before you start, make it home. Make sure all the tools are there — tongs, barbecue gloves or hot pads, meat thermometer, spray bottle, etc. All your seasonings and oils and the main course should be prepped and ready. The more organized you are going in, the more fun you can expect and the more perfection you end up with.

Preheat, preheat, preheat. You will see this in every recipe. We wouldn't keep saying it if it wasn't important. If you can place your hand 5 inches (13 cm) above the grill and hold it there for longer than 5 seconds, the grill isn't ready. Start high and adjust from there. Among other things, this seasons your grill. Food doesn't stick to a properly seasoned and preheated grill.

Food safety is paramount. Be very sure you cook foods to the recommended internal temperatures. This is especially important with poultry and pork. It is not, however, necessary to cook them into oblivion. Good cuts of pork need to be a nice juicy medium, not cooked to dry, grey misery. Chicken needs to be cooked until the pink is gone and the juices are clear, but not until the juices disappear and a sauce is necessary to disguise the dryness.

NEVER put cooked meat on the same surface, plate, or board that had raw meat on it without carefully sanitizing the surface. Food poisoning in the home is always caused by carelessness. Don't send your guests home with a nasty souvenir.

Barbecue sauces and marinades have sugar in them. Brush or wipe marinades off before setting something on the grill. If you are using the marinade as a baste, use it carefully so flare-ups don't cremate the outside before the centre is cooked.

Pay attention to your recipe. It is not always safe to use the marinade for basting. If the recipe says discard then discard. If the recipe says boil it before using then be sure you actually boil it.

Barbecue sauces should be brushed on in the last moments of cooking. Too much sauce too soon will produce only a burnt bitter result. For a roast, you may only need 20 to 30 minutes; for a burger, 2 to 3 minutes. Use judgment.

Don't rush your food. If you try to flip a burger or a piece of meat, and especially a piece of fish, and it doesn't yield easily, it is either not ready to flip or the grill wasn't preheated. Step back and take a deep breath; it will yield to the spatula easily when it is ready. This is not a race.

Use tongs on the grill. You don't want to pierce or tear the foods and lose those precious juices.

Should the lid be up or down? Your Napoleon® grill has a thermometer on the hood. We have endeavoured to tell you when the lid should be up and when it should be down. If you aren't sure, keep an eye on that temperature gauge. If the internal heat of the grill is high, the food is going to be cooking quickly. Sometimes you will want this, and sometimes you will want to adjust the heat. But lowering the hood is always a better way to speed up the cooking without losing the juices and flavours.

Aluminum foil is a necessary tool in your grilling arsenal. Buy the wide, heavy-duty foil (lightweight foil can become downright dangerous around the grill). You can use foil to cover something directly on the grill to focus heat and moisture. You will be wrapping things before, during, and after for various reasons. Elsewhere in the book we discuss cooking with foil packets and pouches. Always remember that hot steam is being produced in these packets and be very careful opening them — steam burns are extremely painful.

Foil is a good way to keep small pieces such as vegetables from falling through the grates if you don't have a Napoleon® Multi-Basket or Napoleon® Griddle. But, we do encourage you to look into some of the accessories available to help you reach new levels of creativity. Though it's quite possible to have a very satisfying grill experience with just the basics, tools like the wok toppers, griddles, and various baskets make the grill zone a supremely gratifying place to be.

You have your shiny Napoleon® grill preheated, the steaks are seasoned and ready to go, and your neighbours are eyeing you with a combination of anticipation and pessimism. Shall we show them how it's done?

TOOLS

Here is a list of what we see as a necessary part of your Napoleon® grill zone:

BARBECUE GLOVES — Absolutely essential, and make sure they are always at hand! I prefer rawhide because, even if they get wet, they won't burn you. Remember, water turns to steam. Wet towels or oven mitts can produce a very bad burn. Gloves with a long sleeve are best for the grill, especially when working with infrared burners.

A MEAT THERMOMETER — A good instant-read or probe thermometer is your friend. The results are never in doubt. Napoleon® has a couple of good ones in its inventory.

TONGS — Not those cheap wobbly things you get at super-markets or those decorator grill ones with so much tension you can't grip them properly. Invest in a set of good, well-made, traditional, long-handled restaurant tongs. You spent a lot on that piece of meat. Do you really want to drop it with a pair of hopeless tongs?

A SPATULA — Not the one your spouse uses to flip fried eggs, but a good wide one with a bit of length that will lift a large but delicate fillet of salmon, for instance.

SKEWERS — Bamboo skewers are great, but they burn and you will always forget to soak them. Get a set of stainless skewers that are flat so they don't roll on the grill.

BRUSHES — For basting, marinating, brushing, etc. The best invention in years is the silicon brush. Have a few on hand. You don't want to dip the brush you are using for cooked meat into the marinade that had raw meat in it.

AN APRON — It's a messy job. If you don't have a chef jacket to get nasty in, an apron is a good thing.

MINIMUM SAFE INTERNAL TEMPERATURES

GROUND MEATS AND MIXTURES

Beef, pork, veal, and lamb	160ºF (70ºC)
Turkey and chicken	165ºF (74ºC)

*Undercooked ground meats can be very unsafe.

BEEF, VEAL, AND LAMB (FRESH)

Medium rare	145ºF (63ºC)
Medium	160ºF (70ºC)
Well done	170ºF (77ºC)

POULTRY

Chicken and turkey, whole	165ºF (74ºC)
Poultry stuffing	160ºF (70ºC)
Poultry breasts	160ºF (70ºC)
Poultry thighs and wings	165ºF (74ºC)

PORK

Medium	150ºF (66ºC)
Well-done	160ºF (70ºC)
Ham (fresh)	160ºF (70ºC)
Ham (precooked, to reheat)	145ºF (63ºC)

RUBS

RIB AND CHICKEN BBQ SEASONING AND RUB

½ cup	sweet paprika	125 mL
¼ cup	chili powder	60 mL
¼ cup	freshly ground black pepper	60 mL
½ cup	kosher salt	125 mL
¼ cup	celery salt	60 mL
¼ cup	granulated sugar	60 mL
2 tbsp	dried sage	30 mL
1 tbsp	dried thyme	15 mL
2 tbsp	onion powder	30 mL
2 tbsp	hot mustard powder	30 mL
2 tsp	cayenne pepper	10 mL
	Zest of 3–4 lemons, minced and air-dried	

• Mix all the ingredients together.

• Store in an airtight container in a cool dry place for up to 3 months.

Makes 2½ cups (625 mL)
Prep Time: 15 minutes

TIP: Chicken benefits from applying the rub both on and under the skin. I like to gently lift the skin and massage a generous bit of the rub right into the meat and then finish by rubbing more over the skin. No matter how well you massage the rub into the skin, it will never penetrate to the meat without this step.

CAJUN CREOLE SEASONING AND RUB

2 tbsp	table salt	30 mL
2 tbsp	sweet paprika	30 mL
2 tbsp	cayenne pepper	30 mL
1 tbsp	granulated sugar	15 mL
1 tbsp	hot mustard powder	15 mL
1 tbsp	freshly ground black pepper	15 mL
1 tbsp	white pepper	15 mL
1 tbsp	garlic powder	15 mL
1 tbsp	onion powder	15 mL
2 tsp	ground cumin	10 mL
1 tsp	dried oregano	5 mL
1 tsp	dried thyme	5 mL
1 tsp	dried rubbed sage	5 mL
1 tsp	ground coriander	5 mL

• Mix all the ingredients together.

• Store in an airtight container in a cool dry place for up to 3 months.

Makes 1 cup (250 mL)
Prep Time: 15 minutes

STEAK SPICE

½ cup	coarse kosher salt	125 mL
¼ cup	coarsely ground black pepper	60 mL
¼ cup	coarsely ground white pepper	60 mL
¼ cup	yellow mustard seeds	60 mL
¼ cup	cracked coriander seeds	60 mL
¼ cup	granulated garlic	60 mL
¼ cup	granulated onion	60 mL
¼ cup	hot pepper flakes	60 mL
¼ cup	dill seed	60 mL

- Mix all the ingredients together.

- Store in an airtight container in a cool dry place for up to 3 months.

Makes 2½ cups (625 mL)
Prep Time: 15 minutes

HOT AND SPICY BBQ SEASONING AND RUB

½ cup	sweet paprika	125 mL
¼ cup	chili powder	60 mL
3 tbsp	salt	45 mL
2 tbsp	ground coriander	30 mL
2 tbsp	garlic powder	30 mL
2 tbsp	granulated sugar	30 mL
2 tbsp	curry powder	30 mL
2 tbsp	hot mustard powder	30 mL
1 tbsp	freshly ground black pepper	15 mL
1 tbsp	dried basil	15 mL
1 tbsp	dried thyme	15 mL
1 tbsp	ground cumin	15 mL
1 tbsp	cayenne pepper	15 mL

- Mix all the ingredients together.

- Store in an airtight container in a cool dry place for up to 3 months.

Makes 2½ cups (625 mL)
Prep Time: 15 minutes

TANDOORI SEASONING AND RUB

¼ cup	ground cumin	60 mL
3 tbsp	turmeric	45 mL
1 tbsp	salt	15 mL
1 tbsp	ground ginger	15 mL
1 tbsp	ground coriander	15 mL
1 tbsp	freshly ground black pepper	15 mL
1 tbsp	mustard powder	15 mL
2 tsp	ground cinnamon	10 mL
2 tsp	hot pepper flakes	10 mL
1 tsp	ground fennel seeds	5 mL
1 tsp	freshly grated nutmeg	5 mL
1 tsp	ground mace	5 mL

- Mix all the ingredients together.
- Store in an airtight container in a cool dry place for up to 3 months.

Makes ¾ cup (175 mL)
Prep Time: 15 minutes

JERK SEASONING AND RUB

2 tbsp	onion powder	30 mL
2 tbsp	ground allspice	30 mL
2 tbsp	cayenne pepper	30 mL
2 tbsp	dried chives	30 mL
1 tbsp	firmly packed brown sugar	15 mL
1 tbsp	freshly ground black pepper	15 mL
1 tbsp	garlic salt	15 mL
1 tbsp	ground habenaro or Scotch bonnet chile	15 mL
1 tbsp	kosher salt	15 mL
1 tsp	mustard powder	5 mL
½ tsp	freshly grated nutmeg	2 mL
¼ tsp	ground cinnamon	1 mL

- Mix all the ingredients together.
- Store in an airtight container in a cool dry place for up to 3 months.

Makes 1 cup (250 mL)
Prep Time: 15 minutes

SEAFOOD SEASONING AND RUB

¼ cup	lemon pepper	60 mL
¼ cup	coarse kosher salt	60 mL
¼ cup	dill seed	60 mL
¼ cup	ground coriander	60 mL
2 tbsp	dried dill	30 mL
1 tbsp	sweet paprika	15 mL
1 tbsp	granulated garlic	15 mL
1 tbsp	granulated onion	15 mL
2 tsp	cayenne pepper	10 mL
2 tsp	granulated sugar	10 mL

- Mix all the ingredients together.
- Store in an airtight container in a cool dry place for up to 3 months.

Makes 1½ cups (375 mL)
Prep Time: 15 minutes

MEMPHIS RIB RUB

1 cup	kosher salt	250 mL
½ cup	firmly packed brown sugar	125 mL
¼ cup	sweet paprika	60 mL
3 tbsp	mustard powder	45 mL
2 tbsp	freshly ground black pepper	30 mL
2 tsp	dried thyme	10 mL
2 tsp	dried marjoram	10 mL
2 tbsp	granulated garlic	30 mL
1 tbsp	granulated onion	15 mL
2 tsp	curry powder	10 mL
2 tsp	ground celery seed	10 mL
1 tsp	cayenne pepper	5 mL

- Mix all the ingredients together.
- Store in an airtight container in a cool dry place for up to 3 months.

Makes 2½ cups (625 mL)
Prep Time: 15 minutes

TIP: Memphis and Kansas City are two well-known styles of BBQ. We could tell you lots of differences and similarities, but to keep it simple, in Memphis the rubs have medium to high heat and you'll see a lot of dry mustard. Memphis supporters also use prepared mustard, a lot of vinegar, and some ketchup in their sauces. In KC the rubs are sweeter, often with a lot of brown sugar and prepared yellow mustard added. KC sauces tend to be tomato-paste-based.

KANSAS CITY RUB

1 cup	firmly packed brown sugar	250 mL
½ cup	sweet paprika	125 mL
3 tbsp	freshly ground black pepper	45 mL
3 tbsp	kosher salt	45 mL
2 tbsp	granulated garlic	30 mL
1½ tbsp	chili powder	22 mL
1½ tbsp	granulated onion	22 mL
1 tbsp	celery salt	15 mL
2 tsp	cayenne pepper	10 mL

- Mix all the ingredients together.
- Store in an airtight container in a cool dry place for up to 3 months.

Makes 2½ cups (625 mL)
Prep Time: 15 minutes

THE BURGER SEASONING!

¼ cup	Hot and Spicy BBQ Seasoning and Rub (see recipe, page 18)	60 mL
1 tbsp	Butter Buds Natural Butter Flavour Granules (available in well-stocked supermarkets and specialty stores)	15 mL
2 tbsp	kosher salt	30 mL
1 tbsp	freshly ground black pepper	15 mL
1 tbsp	dried minced onion	15 mL
1 tbsp	dried minced garlic	15 mL
1 tsp	mustard powder	5 mL
1 tsp	dried chives	5 mL
1 tsp	dried parsley flakes	5 mL

- Mix all the ingredients together.
- Store in an airtight container in a cool dry place for up to 3 months.

Makes 1 cup (250 mL)
Prep Time: 15 minutes

GARLIC AND HERB RUB

2	heads fresh garlic, peeled and minced	2
¼ cup	Steak Spice (see recipe, page 18)	60 mL
¼ cup	finely chopped fresh herbs (parsley, sage, rosemary, thyme, etc.)	60 mL
¼ cup	olive oil	60 mL

- Mix all the ingredients together.
- Store in an airtight container in the refrigerator for up to 3 weeks.

Makes 1¼ cups (300 mL)
Prep Time: 25 minutes

MARINADES

JAMAICAN JERK MARINADE

4	habanero or Scotch bonnet chiles	4
6	green onions, coarsely chopped	6
¼ cup	water	60 mL
1 cup	fresh cilantro	250 mL
1 cup	fresh Italian (flat leaf) parsley	250 mL
6	cloves garlic	6
¼ cup	extra-virgin olive oil	60 mL
¼ cup	freshly squeezed lemon juice	60 mL
2 tbsp	ground allspice	30 mL
2 tsp	kosher salt	10 mL
1 tsp	ground cloves	5 mL
1 tsp	ground cumin	5 mL
1 tsp	freshly ground black pepper	5 mL
2 cups	beer	500 mL
½ cup	granulated sugar	125 mL
¼ cup	kosher salt	60 mL

• In a food processor or blender, purée the chiles, green onions, and water.

• Add cilantro, parsley, and garlic. Process until smooth.

• Pour in olive oil, lemon juice, and seasonings. Process to combine thoroughly.

At this point you have a jerk paste, which will keep, tightly covered, in the refrigerator for 3 weeks.

• Transfer the paste to a nonreactive bowl and whisk in the beer, sugar, and additional salt.

• Cover and refrigerate for up to 3 weeks.

Makes about 4 cups (1 L), or enough to marinate a 5-pound (2.2 kg) boneless pork loin
Prep Time: 25 minutes

TANDOORI MARINADE

¼ cup	sweet paprika	60 mL
2 tbsp	ground cumin	30 mL
1 tbsp	cayenne pepper	15 mL
1 tbsp	ground coriander	15 mL
1 tbsp	ground cardamom	15 mL
1 tbsp	ground cinnamon	15 mL
1 tbsp	freshly ground black pepper	15 mL
1 tsp	ground cloves	5 mL
¼ cup	clarified butter	60 mL
1 tbsp	peeled minced fresh ginger	15 mL
6	cloves garlic, minced	6
2 cups	plain yogurt	500 mL
1 tbsp	freshly squeezed lemon juice	15 mL
2 tsp	salt	10 mL

• In a small bowl, combine the paprika, cumin, cayenne, coriander, cardamom, cinnamon, pepper, and cloves.

• In a frying pan, heat the clarified butter over medium heat. Add the ginger and garlic and sauté, stirring constantly, for 2 to 3 minutes or until fragrant and tender.

• Add the spice blend and continue to sauté for 1 to 2 minutes, allowing the spices to bloom and blend with the garlic and ginger without burning.

• Transfer the spice mixture to a nonreactive bowl. Whisk in the yogurt, lemon juice, and salt and blend thoroughly. Cover and refrigerate for up to 3 weeks.

Makes about 4 cups (1 L), or enough to marinate 4 racks of ribs
Prep Time: 25 minutes

BEER MARINADE

2	bottles beer, such as a pilsner	2
½ cup	freshly squeezed lime juice	125 mL
¼ cup	Hot and Spicy BBQ Seasoning and Rub (see recipe, page 18)	60 mL
8	cloves garlic, minced	8
¼ cup	Worcestershire sauce	60 mL
2 tbsp	soy sauce	30 mL
2 tbsp	extra-virgin olive oil	30 mL
4	serrano chiles, seeded and minced	4
½	bunch fresh cilantro, coarsely chopped	½

- Thoroughly combine all the ingredients in a nonreactive bowl.
- Cover and refrigerate for up to 3 weeks.

Makes about 4 cups (1 L)
Prep Time: 20 minutes

RED WINE MARINADE

2 cups	dry red wine (such as Cabernet Sauvignon or Shiraz)	500 mL
6	cloves garlic, minced	6
2 tbsp	chopped mixed fresh herbs (rosemary, thyme, parsley, etc.)	30 mL
2 tbsp	extra-virgin olive oil	30 mL
1 tbsp	coarsely ground black pepper	15 mL
1 tbsp	balsamic vinegar	15 mL
1 tsp	Worcestershire sauce	5 mL

- Thoroughly combine all ingredients in a nonreactive bowl.
- Cover and refrigerate for up to 1 week.

TIP: Marinades have sugar in them. They should always be brushed off before setting the food on the grill. If you are using it as a baste, to prevent flare-ups, take care in how you use it.

Makes about 2½ cups (625 mL)
Prep Time: 20 minutes

WHITE WINE MARINADE

4	cloves garlic, minced	4
1	green onion, chopped	1
1	red chile, seeded and minced	1
2 cups	dry white wine (such as Chardonnay or Pinot Noir)	500 mL
½ cup	chopped fresh herbs (basil, parsley, thyme, cilantro, etc.)	125 mL
½ cup	freshly squeezed orange juice	125 mL
3 tbsp	extra-virgin olive oil	45 mL
2 tbsp	coarsely ground whole-grain mustard	30 mL
2 tbsp	rice wine vinegar	30 mL
1 tsp	peeled grated fresh ginger	5 mL
1 tsp	coarsely ground black pepper	5 mL

- Thoroughly combine all ingredients in a nonreactive bowl.
- Cover and refrigerate for up to 1 week.

Makes about 2½ cups (625 mL)
Prep Time: 20 minutes

THAI LIME AND CHILE MARINADE

½ cup	coconut milk	125 mL
1	stalk lemongrass, pale green parts crushed and chopped	1
	Juice of 3 limes	
2	small Thai (bird's eye) chiles	2
1 tbsp	peeled, chopped fresh ginger	15 mL
6	cloves garlic, minced	6
2 tbsp	firmly packed brown sugar	30 mL
2 tbsp	vegetable oil	30 mL
1 tsp	cracked black pepper	5 mL

- Thoroughly combine all ingredients in a nonreactive bowl.
- Cover and refrigerate for up to 1 week.

Makes about 1½ cups (375 mL)
Prep Time: 25 minutes

ROASTED GARLIC AND HERB MARINADE

2	heads Grill-Roasted Garlic (see recipe, page 56)	2
1 cup	tomato juice	250 mL
½ cup	white balsamic vinegar	125 mL
¼ cup	chopped fresh basil	60 mL
¼ cup	chopped fresh thyme	60 mL
¼ cup	chopped fresh oregano	60 mL
¼ cup	chopped fresh parsley	60 mL
2 tbsp	extra-virgin olive oil	30 mL
1 tsp	coarse kosher salt	5 mL
1 tsp	cracked black pepper	5 mL
1 tsp	crushed red pepper	5 mL

- In a food processor, purée the Grill-Roasted Garlic.
- Place puréed garlic and remaining ingredients in a nonreactive bowl. Thoroughly combine.
- Cover and refrigerate for up to 1 week.

Makes about 2 cups (500 mL)
Prep Time: 25 minutes

CITRUS MARINADE

1	head garlic, cloves peeled and minced	1
½ cup	freshly squeezed orange juice	125 mL
½ cup	freshly squeezed lime juice	125 mL
¼ cup	freshly squeezed lemon juice	60 mL
¼ cup	vegetable oil	60 mL
3 tbsp	chopped fresh oregano	45 mL
1 tsp	kosher salt	5 mL
1 tsp	freshly ground black pepper	5 mL
½ tsp	ground cumin	2 mL

- Thoroughly combine all ingredients in a nonreactive bowl.
- Cover and refrigerate for up to 1 week.

Makes about 2 cups (500 mL)
Prep Time: 25 minutes

ITALIAN MARINADE

¼ cup	Grill-Roasted Garlic (see recipe, page 56)	60 mL
¼ cup	balsamic vinegar	60 mL
¼ cup	extra-virgin olive oil	60 mL
1 tbsp	cracked black pepper	15 mL
2	hot Italian green peppers or jalapeño peppers, seeded and minced	2
2 tbsp	chopped fresh basil	30 mL

• Thoroughly combine all ingredients in a nonreactive bowl.

• Cover and refrigerate for up to 1 week.

Makes about 1 cup (250 mL)
Prep Time: 25 minutes

TIP: Pay attention to your recipe. It is not always safe to use your marinade for basting. If the recipe says discard, then discard. If it says boil it, be sure you bring it to a full boil.

SAUCES

There are as many barbecue sauces as there are barbecues in North America. Different regions are recognized by their styles. A barbecue sauce may be thick or it may be watery. It generally combines sour, sweet, and spicy ingredients, though there are uncountable variations.

Kansas City–style sauces have a rich, deep, and sweet tomato background. In Memphis they use something a little less sweet though no less complex. In Alabama you will find white barbecue sauces, and in Texas the chile pepper reigns. We say, try them all and then make one of your own.

In this chapter we have tried to show a few of the best-known styles.

MEMPHIS-STYLE BARBECUE SAUCE

3 tbsp	butter, preferably unsalted	45 mL
2 cups	chopped white onion	500 mL
2	cloves garlic, minced	2
2 cups	ketchup	500 mL
1 cup	red wine vinegar	250 mL
½ cup	firmly packed brown sugar	125 mL
¼ cup	prepared yellow mustard	60 mL
½ tsp	Louisiana hot sauce (or any hot pepper sauce will do)	2 mL
¼ cup	Worcestershire sauce	60 mL

Makes about 4 cups (1 L)
Prep Time: 10 minutes
Cook Time: 30 minutes

In Memphis you will often as not get the sauce served on the side as a dip rather than slathered all over your meat — which is also very, very good!

• In a large saucepan, melt the butter over medium heat. Add the onion and sauté for 5 to 6 minutes, or until soft, fragrant, and just beginning to turn golden.

• Add the garlic and continue cooking for another 4 to 5 minutes. Onions should be turning light gold and garlic should not be burnt.

• Stir in the remaining ingredients and reduce the heat to low.

• Cook for 15 to 20 minutes, stirring frequently. Mixture should be thickened but still loose enough to use as a baste if desired. If sauce is too thick, stir in a little water to reach desired viscosity.

• Sauce will keep, refrigerated, for 2 weeks.

KANSAS CITY BARBECUE SAUCE

1 tbsp	canola oil	15 mL
1	medium white onion, finely diced	1
3	cloves garlic, minced	3
1 cup	plum tomatoes, puréed	250 mL
¾ cup	tomato paste	175 mL
¾ cup	cider vinegar	175 mL
½ cup	firmly packed brown sugar	125 mL
2 tbsp	liquid honey	30 mL
3 tbsp	Worcestershire sauce	45 mL
2 tbsp	prepared yellow mustard	30 mL
1 tbsp	celery salt	15 mL
2 tsp	dried rubbed sage	10 mL
1 tsp	dried basil	5 mL
1 tbsp	freshly ground black pepper	15 mL
1½ tbsp	liquid smoke (optional but desirable)	22 mL
½ cup	water	125 mL

• In a large saucepan, heat the oil over medium heat. Add the onion and sauté for 2 to 3 minutes, or until fragrant. Do not allow onion to brown.

• Add the garlic to the pan and continue cooking for another 1 to 2 minutes. Mixture should be soft and fragrant, with no browning.

• Stir in the remaining ingredients and reduce the heat to low.

• Cook for 20 to 30 minutes, stirring frequently, until you reach the desired viscosity. If it gets too thick, use a little warm water to adjust.

• Sauce will keep, refrigerated, for 2 weeks.

Makes about 2½ cups (625 mL)
Prep Time: 15 minutes
Cook Time: 35 minutes

TEXAS-STYLE BARBECUE SAUCE

2 tbsp	butter	30 mL
2	medium onions, finely diced	2
7–10	cloves garlic, minced	7–10
2	serrano chiles, stemmed, seeded, and chopped	2
2	jalapeño peppers, stemmed, seeded, and chopped	2
1 cup	ketchup	250 mL
2 tbsp	Worcestershire sauce	30 mL
¾ cup	strong brewed coffee	175 mL
⅓ cup	fancy molasses	75 mL
¼ cup	balsamic vinegar	60 mL
	Zest and juice of 1 lemon	
2 tbsp	packed brown sugar	30 mL
2 tbsp	prepared yellow mustard	30 mL
2 tbsp	chili powder	30 mL
2 tbsp	finely chopped fresh oregano (or ½ tsp/2 mL dry)	30 mL
2 tsp	liquid smoke (optional)	10 mL
	Juices from barbecue brisket (if available)	

• In a large saucepan, heat the butter over medium heat. Add the onion and sauté for 2 to 3 minutes. Add the garlic and chiles and continue sautéing for an additional 2 to 3 minutes.

• Stir in the remaining ingredients and bring the sauce to a gentle simmer. Reduce the heat to low.

• Cook for 25 to 30 minutes, stirring frequently, until you reach the desired viscosity. If it gets too thick, use a little warm water to adjust.

• Sauce will keep, refrigerated, for 2 to 3 weeks.

TIP: Barbecue sauces should nearly always be brushed on in the last moments of cooking. Sauces, as well as some marinades, have sugar in them. Too much sauce too soon will produce only a burnt, bitter result. For a roast, sauce should be applied only in the last 20 to 30 minutes. For a burger, it might be for only the last 2 or 3 minutes. Use your judgment.

Makes about 3½ cups (875 mL)
Prep Time: 15 minutes
Cook Time: 35 minutes

SOUTH CAROLINA YELLOW MUSTARD BARBECUE SAUCE

1 tbsp	butter	15 mL
1	small onion, finely diced	1
4	cloves garlic, minced	4
2	yellow bell peppers, seeded and diced	2
1 cup	prepared yellow mustard	250 mL
¾ cup	cider vinegar	175 mL
¾ cup	freshly squeezed orange juice	175 mL
½ cup	liquid honey	125 mL
1 tsp	turmeric	5 mL
1 tsp	ground cumin	5 mL
1 tsp	freshly ground black pepper	5 mL
½ tsp	cayenne pepper	2 mL
	Salt to taste	

This is great with fish.

• In a large saucepan, melt the butter over medium heat. Add the onion and sauté for 2 to 3 minutes, or until soft.

• Add the garlic and yellow peppers and continue cooking for another 3 to 4 minutes.

• Stir in the remaining ingredients and bring to a simmer. Reduce the heat to low.

• Cook for 20 to 30 minutes, stirring occasionally, until reduced by one-third.

• Season sauce with salt to taste. Let cool slightly and then purée in a blender or food processor until smooth. Cool.

• Sauce will keep, refrigerated, for 2 weeks.

Makes about 3½ cups (875 mL)
Prep Time: 10 minutes
Cook Time: 40 minutes

ALABAMA WHITE BARBECUE SAUCE

1 cup	ranch dressing	250 mL
1 cup	mayonnaise	250 mL
2 tbsp	lemon juice, preferably freshly squeezed	30 mL
1 tbsp	water	15 mL
1 tbsp	coarsely ground black pepper	15 mL
1 tbsp	Worcestershire	15 mL
1 tbsp	fresh chopped parsley	15 mL
1 tbsp	fresh chopped thyme	15 mL
2 tsp	garlic purée	10 mL
2 tsp	hot pepper sauce	10 mL
	Salt to taste	

Great with Beer-Can Chicken (see recipe, page 239)

• In a bowl, whisk together the ranch dressing, mayonnaise, lemon juice, and water.

• Add the remaining ingredients and whisk until well combined. Thin with additional water if needed.

• Sauce will keep, refrigerated, for up to 2 weeks.

Makes 3 cups (750 mL)
Prep Time: 20 minutes

GOURMET-STYLE BARBECUE SAUCE

2 tbsp	olive oil	30 mL
1	medium white onion, finely chopped	1
8	cloves garlic, minced	8
2	8-oz (227 mL) cans crushed plum tomatoes	2
2	6 oz (170 mL) cans tomato paste	2
4 tbsp	firmly packed brown sugar	60 mL
2 tbsp	Worcestershire sauce	30 mL
2 tsp	mustard powder	10 mL
1½ tsp	cayenne pepper	7 mL
¼ cup	bourbon (any good brand)	60 mL
	Freshly ground black pepper to taste	

• In a large saucepan, heat the oil over medium heat. Add the onion and sauté for 2 to 3 minutes, or until fragrant. Do not allow onion to brown.

• Add the garlic and continue cooking for another 2 minutes. Mixture should be soft and fragrant with no browning.

• Stir in tomatoes, tomato paste, brown sugar, Worcestershire, and mustard. Bring to a simmer and cook for 20 minutes to reduce and thicken.

• Stir in cayenne and bourbon, remove from heat and let cool. If it gets too thick, adjust with a little warm water (or a touch more bourbon).

• Sauce will keep, refrigerated, for 2 weeks.

Makes about 3 cups (750 mL)
Prep Time: 15 minutes
Cook Time: 25 minutes

HOT AND SPICY BARBECUE SAUCE

2 tbsp	butter	30 mL
1	medium white onion, finely chopped	1
1	Scotch bonnet chile, stemmed, seeded, and minced	1
1 cup	prepared chili sauce	250 mL
½ cup	beer	125 mL
¼ cup	freshly squeezed lemon juice	60 mL
2 tbsp	firmly packed brown sugar	30 mL
2 tbsp	soy sauce	30 mL
1 tbsp	Worcestershire sauce	15 mL
2 tsp	prepared yellow mustard	10 mL
2 tsp	chili powder	10 mL
1 tsp	sweet Hungarian paprika	5 mL
½ tsp	hot pepper flakes	2 mL

• In a large saucepan, melt the butter over medium heat. Add the onion and sauté for 2 to 3 minutes, or until soft.

• Add the chile and continue cooking for another 2 to 3 minutes.

• Stir in the remaining ingredients and bring to a simmer. Reduce the heat to low and simmer for 20 to 30 minutes, stirring occasionally, until reduced by about one-third.

• Sauce will keep, refrigerated, for 2 weeks.

Makes about 3 cups (750 mL)
Prep Time: 15 minutes
Cook Time: 35 minutes

HOF BRAU BARBECUE SAUCE
WITH BEER AND GRAINY MUSTARD

1½ cups	prepared hickory smoke–flavoured barbecue sauce	375 mL
1 cup	pilsner beer	250 mL
½ cup	lightly packed brown sugar	125 mL
½ cup	ketchup	125 mL
½ cup	grainy Dijon mustard	125 mL
1 tbsp	Cajun Creole Seasoning and Rub (see recipe, page 17)	15 mL

- In a nonreactive saucepan, whisk together all ingredients.

- Heat just to a simmer, stirring occasionally. If too thick, thin with a little beer.

- Sauce will keep, refrigerated, for up to 3 weeks.

Makes 4 cups (1 L)
Prep Time: 10 minutes
Cook Time: 15 minutes

GRILL-ROASTED GARLIC BARBECUE SAUCE

2 tsp	olive oil	10 mL
1	small onion, finely chopped	1
⅓ cup	Grill-Roasted Garlic (see recipe, page 56)	75 mL
1 cup	liquid honey	250 mL
½ cup	apple juice	125 mL
¼ cup	soy sauce	60 mL
¼ cup	cider vinegar	60 mL
	Salt and freshly ground black pepper to taste	

- In a saucepan, heat the olive oil over medium heat. Add the onion and sauté for 4 to 5 minutes, or until very soft.

- Stir in the Grill-Roasted Garlic and continue cooking for another 2 to 3 minutes, taking care not to burn the garlic or let the mixture get beyond golden brown.

- Stir in the remaining ingredients and bring to a simmer.

- Cook for 5 to 7 minutes, whisking occasionally to blend well. Remove from heat.

- Season sauce with salt and pepper to taste.

- Sauce will keep, refrigerated, for 2 to 3 weeks.

Makes about 2½ cups (625 mL)
Prep Time: 15 minutes
Cook Time: 15 minutes

TANDOORI BARBECUE SAUCE

3 tbsp	butter	45 mL
1	small white onion, minced	1
6	cloves garlic, minced	6
1 tbsp	peeled minced fresh ginger	15 mL
5 tbsp	Tandoori Seasoning and Rub (see recipe, page 21)	75 mL
2 tsp	ground cardamom	10 mL
2 cups	plain yogurt	500 mL
1 tbsp	freshly squeezed lemon juice	15 mL
	Salt to taste	

Use as a marinade for chicken as well.

• In a saucepan, melt the butter over medium heat. Add the onion and sauté for 4 to 5 minutes, or until very soft.

• Add the garlic and ginger to the pan and continue cooking, stirring constantly, for 2 to 3 minutes.

• Add the Tandoori Seasoning and Rub to the pan and continue cooking for another 3 to 4 minutes. Be very careful with the spices at this point. They should become fragrant without burning.

• Remove onion mixture from heat and allow to cool slightly.

• Stir mixture into the cardamom, yogurt, and lemon juice and season with salt.

• Sauce will keep, refrigerated, for 3 to 5 days.

Makes about 3½ cups (875 mL)
Prep Time: 15 minutes
Cook Time: 20 minutes

MANGO BARBECUE SAUCE

3 tbsp	olive oil	45 mL
1	small onion, finely diced	1
1	medium red bell pepper, stemmed, seeded, and finely diced	1
4	cloves garlic, minced	4
3 tbsp	peeled and minced fresh ginger	45 mL
1	jalapeño or serrano chile, stemmed, seeded, and minced	1
4	fresh mangoes, peeled, pitted, and finely diced	4
1 cup	apple cider vinegar	250 mL
1 cup	lightly packed brown sugar	250 mL
2 tbsp	yellow mustard seeds	30 mL
½ tsp	ground allspice	5 mL
½ tsp	ground cinnamon	5 mL

Great with chicken or fish.

• In a large saucepan, heat the olive oil over medium heat. Add the onion and sauté for 4 to 5 minutes, or until very soft.

• Add the red bell pepper, garlic, ginger, and jalapeño and continue cooking for another 3 to 4 minutes.

• Add the mango and continue cooking, slowly stirring to prevent burning, until mango is softened and beginning to break down, about another 5 to 7 minutes.

• Stir in the remaining ingredients and bring to a simmer. Reduce the heat to low. Simmer for 10 to 15 minutes, stirring occasionally, until reduced slightly and thickened.

• Sauce will keep, refrigerated, for 2 weeks.

Makes about 4 cups (1 L)
Prep Time: 15 minutes
Cook Time: 30 minutes

GRILLED VEGETABLES AND FRUIT

We tend to think only of meat when we're at the barbecue. But there is really very little you can't use the grill for. Once the grill is lit, why not throw some veggies on too?

Some vegetables require more preparation than others. But this can be done long before the grill is lit, so with a little planning, you can set up in front of the grill and never leave until it's time to call the crowd to the table.

Grilling is an effective way to concentrate the natural flavours of a vegetable while losing very little of its nutrition. Natural sugars caramelize and enhance those fresh flavours. Add a little seasoning, and impress family and friends. The basic principles apply to most vegetables. Don't be afraid to experiment using some of the simple skills we offer here.

Vegetables are mainly water and most contain no fat. Most require brushing with a little oil, a flavouring marinade with an oil base, or a pouch made of foil or leaves. Oils are available in many hues and flavours, and you can easily create your own. Consider the health benefits of packing vegetables and flavourings into foil or leaf (banana, lettuce, cabbage, etc.) pouches and allowing them to steam alongside that pork loin. Last but certainly not least, baskets, skewers, and grill wok accessories are becoming more and more popular, and they provide even easier ways to cook vegetables on the grill.

Grill-Roasted Corn on the Cob, page 64

BASIC GRILLED VEGETABLES

1–2 cups	prepared vegetables, per person	250–500 mL

Vegetable oil to for brushing the grill rack or Napoleon® Multi-Grill Basket

Flavoured oil or marinade to brush vegetables

Salt and freshly ground black pepper

• Prepare the vegetables by cutting into pieces of approximately even size and thickness.

• Preheat grill to medium (350ºF/175ºC), unless instructed otherwise by a specific recipe. Place a drip pan beneath the rack to prevent flare-ups.

• While grill is preheating, brush or toss the vegetables in flavoured oil or marinade to coat well; season lightly with salt and pepper.

• When the grill is ready, brush the rack or basket with a light coating of vegetable oil to help prevent sticking.

• Place the vegetables directly on the rack or pack in an even layer in the basket. Cook, basting with selected flavouring and turning frequently, until browned and tender. Denser root vegetables will benefit from closing the lid for 3 to 5 minutes at a time to allow the heat to penetrate and roast them.

• Vegetables are done when browned and tender when pierced with a skewer. Take care not to allow the vegetables to burn or overcook and become soft and mushy. The best flavours come from vegetables that are just tender — before the natural sugars have begun to burn.

• Serve. Grilled vegetables are delicious warm or at room temperature.

TIP: Grilled vegetables bring to mind all the toys and tools that enhance the experience. There are Napoleon® Multi-Baskets, Napoleon® Griddles, and wok toppers and various baskets. Foil will help in all sorts of ways but these accessories are motivators to really amp up the grill experience.

Prep Time: 10 to 30 minutes
Cook Time: 10 to 30 minutes

COMMON GRILLING VEGETABLES
AND PREPARATION TIPS FOR GRILLING

Some vegetables are better grilled after some precooking; some are best grilled from raw. Following is a list with preparation instructions and approximate cook times. Keep in mind that these are guidelines and personal preferences will vary from person to person.

ARTICHOKES: Fresh artichokes require cleaning and cooking until just tender before being placed on the grill. Tinned artichokes are also delicious after flavouring and grilling. Cut fresh into halves or quarters; leave tinned whole. Grill time: 5 to 10 minutes.

ASPARAGUS: Remove woody ends and peel lower stems. Asparagus can be grilled either raw or blanched. Blanched or steamed until barely tender, grill time: about 3 to 4 minutes. Soak raw asparagus in water or a marinade for at least 30 minutes to overnight. Grill time: 3 to 7 minutes, depending on thickness of asparagus. Take care not to let ends burn.

BEETS: Steam or boil until barely tender. Cool and peel. Slice into equal-sized pieces ½ to 1 inch (1 to 2.5 cm) thick. Small ones can be left whole or halved. Grill time: 7 to 10 minutes. Beets contain a lot of sugar, so take care, as those sugars will burn very easily.

BELGIUM ENDIVE, RADICCHIO, OR SMALL ROMAINE: Cut into halves or quarters lengthwise, leaving enough of the root intact to hold leaves together. Follow the recipe for Basic Grilled Vegetables (page 53), taking care not to burn the delicate leaves. Grill time: about 5 to 7 minutes.

BROCCOLI: Trim down to equal-sized spears approximately 1½ by 2 inches (4 by 5 cm), peeling any tough stems. Blanch or steam slightly until crisp-tender. Grill time: about 5 to 7 minutes.

CARROTS OR PARSNIPS: Cook until just barely tender. Leave small ones whole; slice large ones on the diagonal or in chunks approximately 1 inch (2.5 cm) thick. Grill time: 9 to 12 minutes.

CAULIFLOWER: As for broccoli, but a whole blanched head can also be cut into wedges about 2 inches (5 cm) wide at the thick side. Grill time: 5 to 7 minutes.

CORN: See recipe, page 64.

EGGPLANT: Leave very small ones whole. Long thin ones, such as Japanese eggplants, should be cut lengthwise in half. Larger ones should be sliced on the diagonal into ½- to 1-inch (1 to 2.5 cm) slices. They can also be cut lengthwise almost to the stem and fanned. Grill time: 13 to 15 minutes. Eggplant will tolerate slightly higher and more direct heat, but take care not to burn.

FENNEL: Cut cleaned bulbs into thick slices (½ to 1 inch/1 to 2.5 cm) or wedges. Grill time: 13 to 15 minutes.

GREEN ONIONS: Slice off roots and trim down dark green ends. Grill time: 7 to 10 minutes.

LEEKS: Trim the root end but leave intact to hold the leek together. Trim the tough dark green tops. Split lengthwise into halves or quarters. Rinse off any soil clinging between the layers. Grill time: 5 to 10 minutes.

MUSHROOMS: See recipe, page 60.

ONIONS: red, white, Vidalia, shallots: Onions can be grilled peeled or unpeeled. If onions are cut into wedges, leave root end trimmed but intact to hold wedge together. If cutting into thick slices, trim root ends off. Leave shallots whole. Grill time for small whole and halved or quartered onions: 15 to 20 minutes. Grill time for thick slices: 5 to 7 minutes.

PEPPERS: bell peppers, chiles, jalapeños: Place peppers on the grill whole and uncut. Grill until evenly charred on all sides. Remove and immediately enclose in a paper bag or place in a bowl and cover tightly with plastic wrap. Let sit for 15 to 20 minutes to steam. Remove from bag or bowl, and rub off skins. Slice lengthwise, stem, seed, and remove membranes. Slice into strips or chunks as preferred. Grill time: 10 to 12 minutes.

POTATOES AND SWEET POTATOES: See recipe, page 63.

RUTABAGAS AND TURNIPS: Peel and slice about ½ to 1 inch (1 to 2.5 cm) thick. Blanch or steam until just tender. Grill time: about 8 to 10 minutes.

SQUASHES: summer and winter: Leave small squashes whole. Cut large ones lengthwise into halves or quarters. Cut zucchini or marrow in half lengthwise into ½-inch (1 cm) slices on the diagonal. Winter squash will need blanching until barely tender. Grill time: 7 to 10 minutes.

TOMATOES: Grill cherry tomatoes whole. Larger tomatoes should be cut into halves or thick slices. The best tomatoes for grilling are firm and slightly underripe or green. Grill time: 8 to 15 minutes.

GRILL-ROASTED GARLIC

4	heads garlic	4	
¼ cup	extra-virgin olive oil	60 mL	

• Preheat grill to medium (350ºF/175ºC).

• Take a sharp knife and slice the top off each head of garlic about one-quarter to one-third of the way down so as to expose some of each clove.

• Place the garlic heads in the centre of a double layer of heavy-duty aluminum foil about 12 by 12 inches (30 by 30 cm) square. Drizzle the heads with olive oil and turn them upside down on the foil, then bring the ends of the foil up to create a pouch. Crimp the ends tightly to seal.

• Place the pouch of garlic on the grill and roast for approximately 1 hour, or until very tender.

• Remove pouch from the grill and carefully unwrap, taking care to let steam escape. Remove garlic cloves from the heads by squeezing gently to pop them out. Use a small fork to dig out any stubborn ones.

• Garlic can be wrapped and stored in refrigerator for 2 weeks or frozen for up to 3 months.

TIP: Spread on grilled breads or flatbread. Mix in sour cream for a roasted garlic dipping sauce for vegetables and chips.

Makes about ½ cup (125 mL)
Prep Time: 5 minutes
Cook Time: 1 hour

ASPARAGUS
WITH RASPBERRIES AND ASIAGO

1	Napoleon® Multi Basket	1
2	bunches asparagus, trimmed and stems peeled	2
2 tbsp	olive oil	30 mL
2 tbsp	raspberry vinegar	30 mL
	Salt and freshly ground black pepper to taste	
1 tbsp	finely chopped fresh thyme	15 mL
1 cup	fresh raspberries	250 mL
¼ cup	Asiago cheese, shredded	60 mL

• Place the asparagus in a large bowl or flat-bottomed cake pan and pour the oil, vinegar, salt, and pepper over. Let sit in marinade for at least 30 minutes to overnight.

• Preheat grill to medium (350ºF/175ºC). Remove asparagus from the marinade and place in a Multi Basket on the grill or place asparagus crosswise on the grill. Cook, turning carefully, until crisp-tender, about 3 to 5 minutes depending on the thickness of the asparagus.

• Return asparagus to the marinade and add the chopped thyme and raspberries. Mix very gently to avoid breaking the spears or crushing the raspberries. Arrange asparagus spears on a serving platter and spoon the raspberries and some of the vinaigrette over.

• Sprinkle the shredded Asiago over the asparagus and serve warm or at room temperature.

Serves 6 to 8
Prep Time: 10 minutes
Marinade Time: 30 minutes to overnight
Cook Time: 5 minutes

TIP: A Napoleon® Multi Basket is especially handy for fruit and vegetables on the grill. It's so much easier to turn one basket than 40 individual asparagus spears. You really can lose your mind picking asparagus spears, mushrooms, or whatever else out from under the grate.

GRILLED MUSHROOMS
WITH ROASTED GARLIC AND GOAT CHEESE

2	large portobello mushroom caps	2
8	large white mushrooms	8
5	large oyster mushrooms	5
4	large shiitake mushroom caps	3
3 cups	very hot water	750 mL
½ cup	balsamic vinegar	125 mL
½ cup	extra-virgin olive oil	125 mL
1 tbsp	Cajun Creole Seasoning and Rub (see recipe, page 17)	15 mL
1	large sweet onion, cut into ½-inch (1 cm) slices	1
1 cup	crumbled goat cheese	250 mL
1½ tbsp	Grill-Roasted Garlic (see recipe, page 56)	22 mL
1 tbsp	fresh basil leaves, sliced	15 mL
	Salt and freshly ground black pepper to taste	
	Extra balsamic vinegar and olive oil for finishing	

• Place the mushrooms in a large bowl and pour the hot water over them. Place a plate on the mushrooms to keep them submerged. Soak mushrooms for 15 minutes (this will keep them from drying out on the grill).

• Drain water and then return mushrooms to the bowl. Add the ½ cup (125 mL) vinegar, ½ cup (125 mL) oil, and seasoning mix, and toss to coat well.

• Preheat grill to medium-high (450ºF/230ºC).

• Remove mushrooms from vinegar mixture, reserving the marinade, and place mushrooms on the grill, top side down. Grill, turning once, for 8 to 12 minutes, or until tender and lightly charred.

• While mushrooms are grilling, brush the onion slices with the vinegar mixture and grill for 8 to 10 minutes, until lightly charred and tender.

• Let mushrooms and onions cool then cut into 1–inch (2.5 cm) chunks. Combine in a bowl with the goat cheese, Grill-Roasted Garlic, and basil. Season to taste with salt and pepper and a few dashes of olive oil and balsamic vinegar.

• Serve at room temperature as a side dish to grilled steaks or pork chops.

Serves 4 to 6
Prep Time: 20 minutes
Marinade Time: 15 minutes to overnight
Cook Time: 25 minutes

TIP: Oyster mushrooms are delicate and will take the least amount of time to cook. Next off will likely be the whites and then the shiitakes. Portobellos are dense and meaty and will take the longest. Always remember multiple cooking times when grilling a variety of items.

GRILLED ROSEMARY POTATOES
WITH LEMON AND OLIVE OIL

6	large red or Yukon gold potatoes, unpeeled, cut into 8 wedges	6
½ cup	extra-virgin olive oil	125 mL
	Juice and finely chopped zest of 2 lemons	
1 tbsp	finely chopped fresh rosemary	15 mL
	Coarse sea salt and freshly ground black pepper to taste	

- Preheat grill to medium-high (450ºF/230ºC).

- Place the potato wedges in a bowl with the olive oil, lemon juice, lemon zest, and rosemary. Toss gently to evenly coat, and season with salt and pepper.

- Remove from the marinade, reserving the marinade, and place the potato wedges in a grill basket or on a perforated rack over the heat.

- Grill in a covered barbecue for approximately 15 minutes a side, or until tender and golden brown. Toss potato wedges in the reserved marinade and adjust the seasoning before serving hot.

Serves 6 to 8
Prep Time: 10 minutes
Marinade Time: 5 minutes to overnight
Cook Time: 30 minutes

HOT AND SPICY GRILLED SWEET POTATOES

3	large sweet potatoes, peeled and cut into ½-inch (1 cm) slices	3
3 tbsp	extra-virgin olive oil	45 mL
2 tbsp	Hot and Spicy BBQ Seasoning and Rub (see recipe, page 18)	30 mL
2 tbsp	vegetable oil	30 mL
2 tbsp	extra-virgin olive oil	30 mL
2 tbsp	freshly squeezed lime juice	30 mL
2 tbsp	roughly chopped fresh cilantro	30 mL

- Place the sweet potato slices in a bowl with the 3 tbsp (45 mL) olive oil and the seasoning, and gently toss to coat well.

- Preheat grill to medium (350ºF/175ºC) and brush rack with vegetable oil.

- Place sweet potato slices in an even layer on grill and cook, turning occasionally, until they are browned and crispy on the outside and tender on the inside, about 10 to 15 minutes.

- Remove to a serving platter or bowl. Toss with the 2 tbsp (30 ml) olive oil and the lime juice and sprinkle with the cilantro. Serve immediately.

Serves 4 to 6
Prep Time: 15 minutes
Cook Time: 20 minutes

GRILL-ROASTED CORN ON THE COB
WITH PARMIGIANO-REGGIANO BUTTER

12	ears peaches and cream corn, with husks still on	12
2 cups	water	500 mL
1½ cups	dry white wine	375 mL
¼ cup	Garlic and Herb Rub (see recipe, page 26)	60 mL
¾ cup	unsalted butter, softened	175 mL
¾ cup	Parmigiano-Reggiano cheese	175 mL
1½ tsp	coarse salt	7 mL
1 tsp	granulated garlic	5 mL
1 tsp	freshly ground black pepper	5 mL

• Pull the husk away from the ears without detaching it. Remove the silk. Pull the husks back up around the cobs and use a small piece of husk to tie and hold in place at the end.

• Pour water, white wine, and the Garlic Herb Rub into a bucket and whisk well to combine.

• Place the husk-jacketed cobs upright in the bucket and weight them with a plate to submerge in the marinade. If more liquid is needed to cover, add water. Soak overnight.

• Prepare the butter by combining it with the cheese, salt, garlic, and pepper in a bowl and stirring vigorously to mix well. Set aside.

• Preheat the grill to medium (350ºF/175ºC). Place the marinated cobs on the grill. Grill for 15 to 18 minutes, turning occasionally. Husks will become quite dark but will pull back easily to reveal the succulent cobs, which should then be brushed liberally with the Parmigiano butter.

• Arrange cobs on a platter using the pulled-back husks as handles. Serve with salt and more of the cheese butter on the side.

Serves 6 to 12
Prep Time: 20 minutes
Marinade Time: overnight
Cook Time: 20 minutes

GRILLED FRUIT

Just a little more food for thought — grilled fruit. Everybody knows you can grill a pineapple. But that barely scratches the surface. You just grilled a whole pork loin to perfection. Nothing could compliment it more than some grilled apple and pear wedges brushed with butter and rum.

You're out there and you've done the meal and you're feeling very satisfied, but there's one more thing. How about dessert? Why not throw some fruit kebabs brushed in butter and sprinkled with cinnamon sugar on the barbecue? Add a little whipped cream and chocolate sauce as dips, and you've got a tasty dessert.

Many fruits are delicious off the grill, and can be used in both simple and complex recipes. The basic steps are very much the same as for vegetables. The elementary composition of most fruits is water and sugar. Grilling fruits concentrates the flavours and caramelizes the sugars for a much richer taste. The result can enhance a main dish, create a unique appetizer, or, of course, create a scrumptious dessert.

The easiest fruits to use are the hard fruits; apples, pears, and pineapple are the best known. Softer fruits, such as peaches, plums, or mangoes, need a certain amount of attention if they're grilled. They will become mushy, and since they tend to have higher sugar contents, they will also burn easily. This shouldn't scare you — just allow a certain amount of caution.

BASIC GRILLED FRUIT

Prepared fruit, cut in half or in large pieces, peeled or unpeeled as preferred

Cold water, to cover

1 tsp   lemon juice per cup of water   5 mL

Melted butter or flavoured oil (walnut, sesame, etc.) to brush fruit or a marinade

Vegetable oil to brush grill rack or Napoleon® Multi-Grill Basket

Seasoning, such as salt or freshly ground black pepper, cinnamon, nutmeg, etc.

• Place the fruit in a container filled with cold water and lemon juice for about 20 to 30 minutes. This will preserve the flavours and juices on the grill.

• Preheat grill to medium (350ºF/175ºC), unless instructed otherwise by a specific recipe. Place a drip pan beneath the rack to prevent flare-ups from marinade and/or dripping juice.

NOTE: Fruit has a high sugar content and some recipes often call for alcohol, which is very flammable, so a little caution will prevent disasters.

• While grill is preheating, remove the fruit from the water bath and brush with butter or flavoured oil or toss in marinade to coat well.

• When the grill is ready, brush the rack or basket with a light coating of vegetable oil to help prevent sticking.

• Place the fruit directly on the rack or pack in an even layer in the basket. Cook, basting with selected flavouring and turning frequently until lightly charred and warmed. Harder fruits will benefit from closing the lid for 3 to 5 minutes to allow the heat to penetrate and allow them to roast a bit.

• Fruit is done when lightly charred and when the hard fruits are tender when pierced with a skewer. Take care not to allow to burn or overcook until they become soft and mushy. The best flavours come from fruits that are just tender and before the natural sugars have begun to burn.

• Grilled fruit is delicious served warm. Try hot strawberry shortcake, grilled kebabs with warm chocolate sauce and whipped cream to dip, grilled banana splits, and so on. Be adventurous.

Prep Time: 10 to 30 minutes
Marinade Time: 30 minutes
Cook Time: 10 to 30 minutes

SIDE DISHES FOR THE GRILL

PLANKED MASHED POTATOES

2	untreated 12-inch Napoleon® cedar planks, soaked overnight	2
8	large Yukon Gold potatoes, peeled and quartered	8
½ cup	table (18%) cream	125 mL
2 tbsp	softened butter	30 mL
⅓ cup	chopped fresh parsley and/or fresh chives	75 mL
	Salt and freshly ground black pepper to taste	

• In a large pot of salted boiling water, cook potatoes until tender, about 15 to 20 minutes. Place in a colander and drain well. Set aside for 10 to 15 minutes to allow excess water to evaporate.

• Meanwhile, combine the cream and butter in the pot and warm slightly.

• Return the potatoes to the pot and mash together with the butter-cream mixture, seasoning with the chopped herbs and salt and pepper. Take care not to overmash — a few lumps are desirable.

• Set aside to cool to room temperature, cover, and refrigerate until needed. (These steps can be done the day before serving.)

• Preheat grill to medium-high (450ºF/230ºC).

• Form the chilled potatoes into uniform, level, mounds on the pre-soaked cedar planks.

• Roast over direct heat for 5 to 10 minutes, or until the potatoes are golden brown and have formed a crisp crust.

• Carefully remove the smoking plank from the barbecue and move potatoes to an unused plank, a heatproof platter, or directly to plates to serve immediately.

TIP: Keep a spray bottle of water handy when plank cooking. If you hear the crackling of a plank about to ignite, a quick dousing will restore order.

Serves 4 to 6
Prep Time: 15 minutes
Pre Cook: 30 minutes
Final Cook Time: 10 minutes

TWICE-BAKED POTATOES

4	large baking potatoes (8–12 oz /250–375 g each)	4
2 tbsp	extra-virgin olive oil	30 mL
1 tbsp	coarse salt	15 mL
1 tbsp	plus more for sprinkling Cajun Creole Seasoning and Rub (see recipe, page 17)	15 mL
¼ cup	softened butter	60 mL
¼ cup	sour cream	60 mL
¼ cup	whipping (35%) cream	60 mL
¼ cup	shredded orange cheddar cheese	60 mL
2 cups	shredded Swiss cheese, divided	500 mL
	Salt and freshly ground black pepper to taste	
8	slices smoky bacon, sliced and cooked crisp	8
1 cup	smoked chicken, diced	250 mL
2	green onions, finely diced	2

• Preheat oven to 450ºF (230ºC).

• Scrub potatoes and pat dry. Place olive oil, salt, and seasoning in a bowl. Add potatoes and toss to coat evenly.

• Place potatoes directly on the rack of the preheated oven and bake until very tender (they should yield easily when squeezed), 45 to 75 minutes, depending on size.

• Cut potatoes in half lengthwise. Carefully scoop out the pulp, leaving a ½-inch (l cm) shell around the edge. Place the shells on a baking sheet, pressing down slightly to flatten the bottoms and balance the shells.

• In a large bowl, mash the potato pulp. Add the butter, sour cream, whipping cream, cheddar, 1 cup (250 mL) of the Swiss cheese, and salt and pepper to taste. Vigorously stir the mixture to combine until light and fluffy. Fold in bacon, chicken, and green onions.

• Fill shells with the potato mixture, piling high. Sprinkle with the remaining Swiss cheese and Cajun Creole Seasoning and Rub. At this point, the stuffed potatoes can be covered and refrigerated for up to 24 hours.

• Preheat a grill or oven to medium-high (450ºF /230ºC) and bake potatoes either on the top rack of the preheated barbecue or in the preheated oven until heated through and lightly browned.

• Drizzle with your favourite barbecue sauce or gravy and serve immediately.

Serves 6 to 8
Prep Time: 30 minutes
Pre Bake Time: 1 hour
Finish Cook Time: 10 to 30 minutes

CREAMED CORN

8- by 12- by 6-inch deep casserole or one that will hold at least 4 qt (4 L), greased

3 tbsp	butter	45 mL
1	medium onion, diced	1
2	cloves garlic, minced	2
¼ cup	all-purpose flour	60 mL
2 cups	chicken stock (homemade or good-quality store-bought)	500 mL
½ cup	whipping (35%) cream	125 mL
5 cups	fresh corn kernels, cut from approximately 8 cobs of Grill-Roasted Corn on the Cob (see recipe, page 64) or frozen	1.25 L
1	14-oz (398 mL) can creamed corn	1
2 cups	processed cheese, cubed	500 mL
1 tbsp	chopped fresh sage	15 mL
	Salt and freshly ground black pepper	
1 cup	fresh bread crumbs	250 mL
¼ cup	freshly grated Parmesan cheese	60 mL

An excellent brunch or lunch dish with the addition of smoked or grilled chicken.

• In a large pot, melt butter over medium heat. Add onion and sauté for 3 to 4 minutes. Add garlic and continue sautéing for another 2 to 3 minutes, until translucent and fragrant.

• Stir in flour and cook, constantly stirring, until flour begins to brown.

• Add the chicken stock, ½ cup (125 mL) at a time, whisking constantly, and bring to the boil. Reduce heat to a simmer and cook sauce for 10 to 15 minutes, stirring occasionally. Remove from heat when thick and smooth; whisk in cream.

• Add corn, creamed corn, cubed cheese, sage, and salt and pepper to taste. Mix well.

• Preheat oven to 350ºF (175ºC).

• Pour corn into prepared casserole. Top with bread crumbs and Parmesan cheese.

• Bake in preheated oven for 20 to 25 minutes, or until top is golden brown and crisp. Serve immediately.

TIP: Casserole can be prepared, without crumb and Parmesan topping, a day ahead, wrapped, and refrigerated. Preheat oven as above and bake for 30 to 40 minutes. Top with the crumbs and Parmesan and bake an additional 10 to 15 minutes, or until top is golden brown and crisp. Serve immediately.

Serves 6 to 8
Prep Time: 45 minutes
Cook Time: 25 minutes

BARBECUE BAKED BEANS

2 lbs	dry navy beans, soaked overnight in water and drained	900 g
3	cloves garlic, minced	3
1	large white onion, finely diced	1
2	poblano chiles, seeded and diced	2
1 cup	double-smoked bacon, diced	250 mL
1 cup	fancy molasses	250 mL
1 cup	prepared chili sauce	250 mL
½ cup	firmly packed brown sugar	125 mL
1 tbsp	Worcestershire sauce	15 mL
1 tbsp	Dijon mustard	15 mL
2 tsp	salt	10 mL

• Place beans in a large heavy pot or ovenproof crock and cover with cold water.

• Bring to a boil, reduce heat to low, and simmer, stirring occasionally, until the beans are just tender (1 to 1½ hours).

• Preheat oven to 325ºF (160ºC).

• Add remaining ingredients to pot and stir to combine thoroughly.

• Cover and place in oven for 3 hours, stirring every 30 minutes. Beans will become very tender and fragrant.

• Remove cover and cook for 1 more hour.

• Store in the refrigerator for 5 to 7 days or freeze for up to 3 months.

• Reheat beans in a 325ºF (160ºC) oven for 45 to 60 minutes. They can also be reheated in a heavy crock set on the back of a preheated medium (350ºF/175ºC) grill. Remember to stir occasionally.

Makes 15 to 20 servings
Prep Time: 30 minutes
Cook Time: 4 hours
Reheat Time: 1 hour

BAKED SWEET POTATOES
WITH MAPLE BUTTER

4	large sweet potatoes	4
¼ cup	unsalted butter, softened	60 mL
¼ cup	pure maple syrup	60 mL
2 tbsp	roughly chopped fresh thyme	30 mL
	Salt and freshly ground black pepper	

Serves 4 to 6
Prep Time: 10 minutes
Cook Time: 60 minutes

• Preheat grill to medium (350ºF/175ºC).

• Place sweet potatoes on top rack of preheated grill, close lid, and roast for 45 to 60 minutes, or until flesh is soft, and when pierced to the centre, a fork encounters no resistance.

• While sweet potatoes are roasting, combine butter, maple syrup, and thyme and mix to a smooth paste. Season to taste with salt and pepper and set aside.

• Remove sweet potatoes from the grill and split lengthwise, about halfway into the flesh.

• Taking care — the potatoes are hot! — firmly grip by each end and squeeze and push to the centre at the same time. Flesh will balloon up and slightly out.

• Place about 1 tablespoon (15 mL) of the butter mixture in each split potato, pushing lightly down into the flesh.

• Serve immediately and enjoy!

GRILLED CHEESE BAGUETTE
WITH ROASTED GARLIC AND HERB BUTTER

1 cup	salted butter, softened	250 mL
¼ cup	freshly grated Parmesan cheese	60 mL
¼ cup	Grill-Roasted Garlic (see recipe, page 56)	60 mL
2 tbsp	roughly chopped mixed fresh herbs (parsley, sage, thyme, basil, oregano, rosemary, etc.)	30 mL
1 tbsp	roughly chopped fresh chives	15 mL
1 tsp	freshly ground black pepper	5 mL
2	baguettes, cut in half lengthwise	2
1 cup	shredded sharp cheese, such as old cheddar or a good Gruyère	250 mL

Serves 6 to 8
Prep Time: 30 minutes
Cook Time: 45 minutes

• Preheat grill to medium (350ºF/175ºC).

• Place butter, Parmesan, Grill-Roasted Garlic, herbs, chives, and pepper in a food processor and purée until smooth. Take care to combine well without over-processing and beginning to melt the butter.

• Spread the cheese butter generously on cut sides of the baguettes. Place the halves together and wrap each loaf tightly in foil. Place the loaves on top rack of the preheated grill and close lid for 30 minutes.

• Carefully unwrap the bread. Sprinkle each unwrapped half with ¼ cup (60 mL) of the shredded cheese and set back on the top rack of the grill. Close lid for 3 to 4 minutes to allow cheese to melt and brown slightly.

• Slice and arrange on a platter. Serve warm.

LOUISIANA COLLARD GREENS

1	bunch collard greens	1
2 tbsp	kosher salt	30 mL
2 tbsp	vegetable oil	30 mL
1	medium onion, diced	1
6	cloves garlic, minced	6
2	jalapeño peppers, seeded and diced	2
¼ cup	chicken stock	60 mL
2 tbsp	corn syrup	30 mL
2 tbsp	cider vinegar	30 mL
2 tbsp	butter	30 mL
	Salt and freshly ground black pepper to taste	

• Cut the tough stems and ribs off the collard greens and discard. Wash the greens very thoroughly in lots of cold water to remove grit and sand.

• Stack leaves in piles of 2 or 3 and roll into a cigar shape. Thinly slice the rolls to produce a chiffonade of collard greens.

• Wash the sliced greens in cold water one more time (these greens can be very sandy) and drain well. Place greens in a bowl and toss with the salt. Let sit for 15 minutes. Rinse under cold water and drain well (a lettuce spinner is handy here).

• In a large deep skillet, heat the oil over medium high heat. Sauté the onion for 2 to 3 minutes, then add the garlic and jalapeños and sauté for an additional 2 to 3 minutes, until the onion is translucent and the garlic and chile are fragrant.

• Add the collard greens and chicken stock and bring to a boil. Reduce heat, and simmer the greens for 10 minutes, allowing moisture to boil away. Stir in corn syrup, vinegar, and butter.

• Season to taste with salt and black pepper and serve immediately.

Serves 4 to 6
Prep Time: 25 minutes
Cook Time: 25 minutes

SOUTHERN CORNBREAD
WITH BACON AND CHEDDAR

½ lb	sliced bacon, diced, cooked crisp, and drained (fat reserved)	250 g
2 tbsp	bacon fat	30 mL
1½ cups	stone-ground cornmeal	375 mL
½ cup	all-purpose flour	125 mL
2 tbsp	granulated sugar	30 mL
2 tsp	baking soda	10 mL
1 tsp	baking powder	5 mL
1 tsp	salt	5 mL
pinch	cayenne pepper	pinch
3	large eggs	3
1½ cups	buttermilk	375 mL
3 tbsp	melted butter	45 mL
½ cup	grated old cheddar	125 mL

• Preheat grill to high (500ºF/260ºC).

• Place the bacon drippings in a 9- or 10-inch (28 or 30 cm) cast iron skillet and place the pan on the preheated grill. Close the lid and heat to smoking.

• In a large bowl, stir together the cornmeal, flour, sugar, baking soda, baking powder, salt, and cayenne.

• In a smaller bowl, whisk the eggs and buttermilk.

• Pour the wet into the dry ingredients and stir gently until just barely combined (some dry streaks will likely remain). Pour in the butter and add the bacon and cheddar. Mix just enough to distribute through the batter.

• Pour the batter carefully into the smoking skillet and return it to the grill. Close the lid and turn off the burner directly underneath the pan (indirect baking).

• Grill/bake for about 18 minutes, or until light golden brown and a toothpick inserted into the centre of the cornbread comes out clean.

• Cut in wedges and serve hot, straight from the pan. Delicious with honey and butter.

Serves 6
Prep Time: 15 minutes
Cook Time: 30 minutes

GRILLED CORN RISOTTO
WITH ROSEMARY, BABY SPINACH, AND ASIAGO

7 cups	chicken broth, freshly homemade, store-bought or made from a good base	1.75 L
2 cups	extra chicken broth, just in case it's needed	500 mL
3 tbsp	butter	45 mL
1	medium onion, finely diced	1
2	cloves garlic, minced	2
3 cups	grilled corn kernels, cut from approximately 6 cobs (see recipe, page 64)	750 mL
3 tsp	fresh rosemary, chopped, divided	15 mL
2 cups	Arborio rice	500 mL
½ cup	dry white wine	125 mL
4 cups	packed baby spinach leaves	1 L
½ cup	whipping (35%) cream	125 mL
½ cup	freshly grated Parmesan cheese	125 mL
	Salt and freshly ground black pepper to taste	
⅓ cup	freshly grated Asiago cheese	75 mL

Not the traditional method for risotto. But this method works very well for those who have struggled to make a perfect risotto. Follow the instructions precisely.

• Bring the 7 cups (1.75 L) of chicken broth just to the boil. Turn heat to low, cover, and hold until needed.

• In a large heavy pot, melt butter over medium heat. Sauté onion for about 4 to 5 minutes, or until translucent. Add garlic and sauté for another 2 to 3 minutes. Add corn and 2 tsp (10 mL) of the rosemary. Stir and heat for 3 to 4 minutes, ensuring that the butter coats everything.

• Add the rice and stir well for 2 to 3 minutes to blend the ingredients and coat the rice with the butter.

• Add the wine and simmer for about 1 minute, until the wine has evaporated.

• Add the 7 cups of hot stock all at once and stir well for 30 seconds. Bring to the boil, reduce heat, and let simmer uncovered, until rice is just tender, stirring occasionally, about 15 to 18 minutes. Risotto should be creamy and a bit soupy. Add more broth, ¼ cup (60 mL) at a time, if risotto doesn't seem creamy enough. Take care not to overcook — the rice should be tender but not mushy.

• Stir in baby spinach leaves, cream, and Parmesan cheese. Season to taste with salt and pepper.

• Transfer risotto to a serving bowl and sprinkle with the Asiago and remaining rosemary.

Serves 4 as a main course, 6 to 8 as a side dish
Prep Time: 30 minutes
Cook Time: 45 minutes

GRILLED CREAMED ONIONS AND MUSHROOMS

BÉCHAMEL SAUCE

⅓ cup	butter	75 mL
½ cup	all-purpose flour	125 mL
6 cups	whole milk	1.5 L
1	small onion, quartered	1
2	cloves garlic	2
1	bay leaf	1
1 tsp	mustard powder	5 mL
1 tsp	salt	5 mL
pinch	grated nutmeg (fresh if you have it)	pinch
½ cup	whipping (35%) cream	125 mL
	Salt and white pepper to taste	

6	slices thick-cut double-smoked bacon, sliced into ½-inch (1 cm) strips	6
4	cloves garlic, minced	4
2–3	large white onions, sliced, grilled, and cut into 1-inch (1 cm) chunks as for grilled vegetables (see page 54)	2–3
2–3 cups	assorted mushrooms, grilled and sliced or quartered as for grilled vegetables (see page 54)	500–750 mL
¼ cup	crisp white wine, such as Riesling	60 mL
1½ cups	Béchamel Sauce	375 mL
½ cup	whipping (35%) cream	125 mL
	Salt and freshly ground black pepper to taste	
1 cup	shredded Bibb lettuce	250 mL
¼ cup	freshly grated Parmesan cheese	60 mL

• In a heavy pot, melt butter over medium heat. Add the flour and stir to a smooth paste.

• Continue stirring and cooking the roux for 5 minutes, then add the milk, 1 cup (250 mL) at a time, whisking constantly to blend and remove any lumps.

• Add the onion, garlic, bay leaf, mustard, salt, and nutmeg while continuing to gently stir or whisk to prevent scalding or burning the milk. Whisk in the cream and bring the mixture just to a gentle simmer. Cook, stirring constantly, until thickened, smooth, and shiny.

• Pour sauce through a sieve. Adjust salt, pepper, and nutmeg. If not using immediately, place wax paper directly onto surface of sauce to prevent a skin forming. Cool to room temperature, cover, and refrigerate for up to 5 days.

• Heat a large heavy-bottomed pot over medium heat. Add the bacon and sauté for 4 to 5 minutes. Add garlic and continue cooking for an additional 2 to 3 minutes, or until garlic is fragrant but not burned and bacon is crisping.

• Add the grilled onion and mushrooms, and stir the mixture to combine and heat through.

• Stir in the white wine, then the béchamel and cream. Bring just to a gentle boil and allow to simmer, stirring frequently, until the mixture is thick and creamy, about 10 to 15 minutes. If mixture becomes too thick, add more cream and/or wine. Adjust seasoning with salt and pepper and remove from heat.

• Stir in the shredded lettuce and Parmesan. Serve immediately.

Serves 6 to 8
Prep Time: 45 minutes
Cook Time: 25 minutes

FOIL-ROASTED VEGETABLES
WITH GARLIC AND FRESH HERBS

1 cup	shelled fresh or frozen green peas	250 mL
2 cups	small zucchini, halved lengthwise and sliced on the diagonal into 1-inch (2.5 cm) pieces	500 mL
1 cup	thin asparagus, cut in 1-inch (2.5 cm) pieces	250 mL
16	shallots, peeled and halved	16
12	shiitake mushrooms, stemmed and halved or quartered	12
4 cloves	garlic, thinly sliced	4
¼ cup	cider vinegar	60 mL
3 tbsp	extra-virgin olive oil	45 mL
2 tbsp	chopped assorted fresh herbs (thyme, rosemary, oregano, basil, etc.)	30 mL
	Sea salt and freshly ground black pepper	

Any vegetable that can be steamed can be sealed into a foil packet and cooked alongside the meat. The principles in the following recipe will work with any combo of vegetables and seasoning.

• Preheat grill to medium-high (450ºF/230ºC)

• In a large bowl, toss all the ingredients together, gently but thoroughly, making sure that all the vegetables are coated with oil.

• Tear 4 (8- by 12-inch/20- by 30-cm) sheets of heavy-duty aluminum foil and lay them shiny side down. Place one-quarter of the vegetable mixture on each piece, fold over, and completely seal the edges of each packet.

• Place the packets on the preheated grill and close lid. Roast for 16 to 18 minutes, turning once or twice. Sizzling sounds should be heard from inside the packets after about 10 minutes.

• Each packet will serve 2.

Serves 8
Prep Time: 20 to 30 minutes
Cook Time: 20 minutes

TIP: Prep the packets as much as 6 to 8 hours ahead and hold them in the refrigerator until about 30 minutes before grilling.

TIP: Aluminum foil is a necessary tool in your grilling arsenal. Buy the wide heavy-duty foil (lightweight foil can be downright dangerous around the grill). You will use foil to cover foods on the grill to focus heat or hold moisture. You will wrap foods before, during, and after cooking. Remember to be careful; when you seal in moisture you make steam. Always open foil packets carefully. Steam burns are particularly painful.

BARBECUE-FRIED RICE

Napoleon® Round or Square Wok Topper
    or cast iron wok

3 tbsp	vegetable oil	45 mL
½ cup	double-smoked bacon, diced	125 mL
1	medium white onion, thinly sliced	1
1 tbsp	minced garlic	15 mL
½ cup	shiitake mushrooms, stemmed and sliced	125 mL
½ cup	sugar snap peas	125 mL
½ cup	grilled or frozen corn kernels	125 mL
½ cup	finely chopped assorted grilled vegetables	125 mL
1 lb	barbecued meat, such as shredded chicken or pulled pork	500 g
2 cups	cooked white rice	500 mL
¼ cup	soy sauce	60 mL
2 tbsp	sambal oelek (Indonesian chili sauce)	30 mL
3 tbsp	rice wine vinegar	45 mL
3 tbsp	hoisin sauce	45 mL
1 tsp	blended sesame oil	5 mL
4	green onions, sliced	4

• Heat wok over high heat, either directly on the grill grid or on the stove. Once wok is smoking hot, add the oil, bacon, onion, and garlic and sauté for 1 to 2 minutes, until the onion has softened. Toss in the mushrooms and sugar snap peas and continue sautéing for another 1 to 2 minutes.

• Toss in the corn, then the grilled vegetables and barbecued meat, stirring after each addition. Add the cooked rice and mix well.

• Add the soy sauce, sambal oelek, rice wine vinegar, and hoisin sauce. Mix well to thoroughly coat the rice mixture and continue to cook over high heat until any excess liquid has nearly all been absorbed by the rice.

• Sprinkle in the sesame oil and the green onions, stir to distribute the flavours, and serve.

Serves 8
Prep Time: 45 minutes
Cook Time: 10 minutes

APPETIZERS

CEDAR-PLANKED BRIE CHEESE WITH BERRIES

Untreated Napoleon® 12-inch cedar plank, soaked for at least 12 hours

1 tbsp	unsalted butter	15 mL
1	jalapeño pepper, finely chopped	1
3	shallots, thinly sliced	3
	Salt and freshly ground black pepper	
½ cup	seedless raspberry jam	125 mL
¼ cup	white wine	60 mL
2	green onions, thinly sliced	2
2 cups	berries (strawberries, raspberries, blackberries, blueberries, etc.), cleaned (large berries cut into bite-size chunks)	500 mL
2	small wheels of Brie cheese, each about 4 oz (125 g)	2

• In a medium saucepan, heat the butter over medium-high heat. Sauté the jalapeño and shallots in the butter for 1 to 2 minutes, until tender. Season with salt and black pepper to taste. Add the raspberry jam and wine, stirring until jam has melted and liquid is combined. Remove from heat and very gently fold in the green onions and berries. Set aside to cool completely.

• Evenly space the Brie wheels on the pre-soaked plank. Spoon the berry mixture over the top of the two wheels of cheese, being sure to load it on.

• Preheat the barbecue to medium-high (450ºF/230ºC).

• Place the planked Brie on the preheated barbecue and close the lid. Bake for 5 minutes. You want the wood to get hot and start to crackle. If the wood catches fire, use a spray bottle of water to put out the flames.

• Carefully open lid and check the cheese. It is ready when the sides are bulging and it is becoming golden brown. Take care not to leave it until the cheese bursts, or the liquid insides will run out, off the plank, and into the fire.

• Remove planked cheese from the barbecue. Serve with slices of fresh baguette and/or crackers and plenty of napkins.

Serves 6
Prep Time: 20 minutes
Cook Time: 15 minutes

TIP: Set up the Brie and berries on the planks. Cover lightly with plastic wrap and set aside up to 2 hours before grilling.

SWEET AND SPICY GRILLED SHRIMP SKEWERS
WITH PEANUT SAUCE

8 wooden skewers, soaked in cold water overnight

MARINADE

½ cup	extra-virgin olive oil, divided	125 mL
1	small red onion, finely chopped	1
2	jalapeño peppers, stemmed, seeded, and finely chopped	2
3	cloves garlic, minced	3
¼ cup	honey mustard	60 mL
¼ cup	freshly squeezed lemon juice	60 mL
16	dried apricots, halved	16
16	jumbo shrimp (6–8 to the lb/14–18 to the kg)	16
8	green onions, cut in half	8

MARINADE: Four to 6 hours before serving, heat a sauté pan over medium-high heat. Add 2 tbsp (30 mL) of the oil to the pan and sauté the red onion for 2 to 3 minutes, or until translucent. Add the jalapeño and garlic and sauté for a further 2 to 3 minutes, or until tender and fragrant but not browned. Place the onion mixture in a bowl with the rest of the olive oil. Add the mustard and lemon juice and whisk. Let cool to room temperature.

• Place shrimp, apricots, and green onions in the marinade and toss to coat. Cover and refrigerate for 3 to 4 hours, tossing occasionally.

• Preheat grill to medium-high (450ºF/230ºC).

• Thread 2 pieces of apricot, 2 shrimp, and 2 pieces of green onion on each of the soaked skewers. Place on the grill for 3 to 4 minutes a side, basting with the marinade. Discard remaining marinade when skewers are done (when shrimp have just turned deep pink).

• Arrange on a platter with peanut sauce or honey mustard on the side.

TIP: Shrimp can be prepped, marinated, and placed on the skewers no more than, but up to, 24 hours ahead. Wrap and refrigerate until 30 minutes before grilling.

Serves 8 as an appetizer, 4 as a main course
Prep Time: 30 minutes
Marinade Time: 4 hours
Cook Time: 8 to 10 minutes

¼ cup	chunky peanut butter	60 mL
¼ cup	warm water	60 mL
¼ cup	unsweetened coconut milk	60 mL
2 tbsp	rice vinegar	30 mL
2 tbsp	soy sauce	30 mL
2 tbsp	sweet rice wine (mirin) or dry sherry	30 mL
1 tbsp	chopped fresh cilantro	15 mL
½ tsp	toasted sesame oil	2 mL
	Juice of 1 lime	
2	cloves garlic, minced	2
1	red chile, seeded and minced	1
1 tbsp	vegetable oil	15 mL
	Salt and freshly ground black pepper	

PEANUT SAUCE: Microwave peanut butter on High for 10 to 20 seconds to soften.

• Place in the bowl of a food processor or whisk together the softened peanut butter, warm water, coconut milk, rice vinegar, soy sauce, rice wine, cilantro, sesame oil, lime juice, garlic, and chile.

• Slowly add oil in a stream while processing or constantly whisking to form a smooth emulsion. Whisk in additional warm water, 1 tsp (5 mL) at a time, if sauce is too thick. Season with salt and pepper.

• Refrigerate until needed. Keeps, covered, in the refrigerator up to 10 days.

Makes 1 cup (250 mL)
Prep Time: 20 minutes

CHICKEN SATAY

24	wooden or metal skewers, soaked in warm water for at least 2 hours	24
4	boneless skinless chicken breasts (about 6 oz/175 g each)	4

MARINADE

¼ cup	rice wine vinegar	60 mL
2 tbsp	soy sauce	30 mL
1 tbsp	toasted sesame oil	15 mL
1 tbsp	chopped fresh ginger	15 mL
1 tbsp	chopped garlic	15 mL
1 tsp	curry powder	5 mL
1 tsp	freshly ground black pepper	5 mL

• Slice each chicken breast lengthwise into six thin strips, about 1 oz (30 g) each. Carefully thread each strip onto the end of one skewer.

MARINADE: In a flat glass dish large enough to hold the skewers, whisk together the vinegar, soy sauce, sesame oil, ginger, garlic, curry powder, and pepper.

• Add the skewers and turn to coat the chicken in the marinade. Cover and refrigerate for at least 4 to 6 hours, turning occasionally.

• Preheat grill to medium-high (450°F/230°C).

• Remove skewers from the marinade and discard the marinade. Place the skewers on the preheated grill for 2 to 3 minutes a side, or until fully cooked. Serve with Peanut Sauce (see recipe, page 92).

Makes 24 skewers
Serves 6 to 20 as part of an hors d'oeuvres service
Prep Time: 30 minutes
Cook Time: 8 minutes

TIP: Chicken skewers can be prepared no more than, but up to, 24 hours ahead. Remove from the marinade after 4 to 6 hours, wrap and refrigerate until 30 minutes before grilling.

LAMB SPEIDINI

12 to 16 small metal skewers or bamboo skewers, soaked in water for 30 minutes and drained

MARINADE

¼ cup	pomegranate molasses (available at Middle Eastern markets and specialty stores)	60 mL
½ cup	extra-virgin olive oil	125 mL
3	cloves garlic, minced	3
1 tbsp	chopped fresh oregano	15 mL
	Salt and freshly ground black pepper to taste	
1 tsp	ground cinnamon	5 mL
2 tsp	ground cumin	10 mL
1½ lb	boneless leg of lamb, trimmed and cut into ¾- to 1-inch (2 to 2.5 cm) cubes	750 g

MARINADE: In resealable bag, mix pomegranate molasses, oil, garlic, oregano, salt, pepper, cinnamon, and cumin.

• Add lamb and mix; chill for at least 2 or up to 12 hours.

• Remove lamb from marinade. Thread 6 to 8 pieces of lamb on each skewer, being careful not to jam too tightly together. Cover and refrigerate until needed (no more than 6 hours).

• Preheat grill to medium-high (450ºF/230ºC).

• Sprinkle kebabs with salt and pepper to taste. Cook, turning often, about 4 minutes for medium-rare.

• Serve on a platter with a little extra molasses drizzled over.

Serves 6 to 8 as an appetizer
Prep Time: 30 minutes
Cook Time: 4 to 5 minutes

FIRE-ROASTED TOMATO AND ONION BRUSCHETTA

8	ripe plum tomatoes, sliced in half lengthwise	8
2	medium red onions, peeled and thickly sliced	2
¼ cup	olive oil	60 mL
	Salt and freshly ground black pepper to taste	
3 tbsp	olive oil	45 mL
2 tbsp	chopped fresh curly parsley	30 mL
2 tbsp	chopped fresh basil	30 mL
3 tbsp	Grill-Roasted Garlic (see recipe, page 56)	45 mL
2 tbsp	balsamic vinegar	30 mL
	Finely chopped zest (approx 1 tbsp/15 mL) and juice of 1 lemon	
	Salt and freshly ground black pepper	
1	fresh baguette, 16 to 18 inches (28 to 30 cm) long, sliced on the diagonal into ¾-inch (2 cm) slices	1
½ cup	freshly grated Parmesan cheese	125 mL

• Preheat the grill to medium (350ºF/175ºC).

• Toss the tomatoes and red onion in the ¼ cup (60 mL) oil and season with salt and pepper. Grill until lightly charred and tender, 7 to 10 minutes (tomatoes will be done before the onions).

• Finely dice tomatoes and onions with a very sharp knife. Combine in a bowl with the 3 tbsp (45 mL) oil, parsley, basil, Grill-Roasted Garlic, balsamic vinegar, and lemon zest and juice. Mix well, taking care not to crush the tomatoes to pulp. Season to taste with salt and pepper. Set aside.

• Grill baguette slices 1 to 2 minutes a side, or until lightly browned and crisp. Place a heaping spoonful of the tomato and onion topping on each slice. Sprinkle with Parmesan cheese and serve.

Makes approximately 20 to 24 bruschetta. Serves 6 to 20 as part of an hors d'oeuvres service.
Prep Time: 45 minutes
Cook Time: 5 minutes

CHICKEN QUESADILLAS WITH GRILLED CORN, MONTEREY JACK, CHILE, AND FIRE-ROASTED SALSA

3	boneless skinless chicken breasts (about 6 oz/175 g each)	3
2 tbsp	Cajun Creole Seasoning and Rub (see recipe, page 17)	30 mL
1 cup	Grill-Roasted Garlic Barbecue Sauce (see recipe, page 47), divided	250 mL
1½ cups	grilled corn (see page 64) or 12 oz (375 mL) frozen corn kernels	375 mL
3	cloves garlic, minced	3
1	small red onion, peeled and diced	1
1	jalapeño pepper, seeded and finely diced	1
1	yellow or red bell pepper, diced	1
1 tbsp	chopped fresh cilantro	15 mL
	Salt and freshly ground black pepper to taste	
2 cups	shredded Monterey Jack cheese	500 mL
1 cup	shredded cheddar cheese	250 mL
8	7-inch (18 cm) flour tortillas	8
	Olive oil	

• Preheat grill to medium-high (450ºF/230ºC).

• Rub chicken breasts with Cajun Creole Seasoning and Rub. Grill chicken, basting with ½ cup (125 mL) of the Grill-Roasted Garlic Barbecue Sauce, 5 to 6 minutes per side, or until fully cooked. Let cool and slice thinly against the grain. Set aside.

• Combine corn, garlic, onion, jalapeño, bell pepper, cilantro, ¼ cup (60 mL) of the Grill-Roasted Garlic Barbecue Sauce, and salt and pepper to taste.

• Leaving a ½-inch (1 cm) border around edge, brush 4 tortillas with the remaining ¼ cup (60 mL) of barbecue sauce. Mix the cheeses together and sprinkle one-quarter evenly over each tortilla. Spread 2 tbsp (30 mL) of the corn mixture evenly over the cheese. Top with one-quarter of chicken, then divide remaining corn salsa and cheese between the tortillas. Moisten edges of tortillas by brushing liberally with water and then top with remaining tortillas, pressing edges to seal.

• Preheat grill to medium (350ºF/175ºC).

• Brush each quesadilla lightly on both sides with olive oil. Grill 2 to 3 minutes a side, until lightly charred and crisp, and cheese melts.

• Remove from grill and let sit for 5 minutes. Cut each quesadilla into 8 wedges and serve with the Fire-Roasted Salsa.

TIP: Make Quesadillas 4 to 6 hours ahead of grill time. Wrap and refrigerate until 30 minutes before grilling.

TIP: If planning a large backyard cocktail-style barbecue where you will serve only passed and plattered appetizers, expect to need 6 to 8 pieces per person. But more like 10 to 12 if you are covering a meal period. Think about what favourite grill dishes you do that can be miniaturized: mini burgers, ribs cut in singles and so on. Don't forget lots of napkins and wet wipes.

Makes 32 wedges. Serves 8 to 24 as part of an hors d'oeuvres service.
Prep Time: 45 minutes
Cook Time: 6 minutes

1	large onion, thickly (¾ inch/2 cm) sliced	1
4	plum tomatoes, sliced in half lengthwise	4
2	cloves garlic, minced	2
¼ cup	chopped mixed fresh herbs (cilantro, thyme, basil, parsley, etc.)	60 mL
½ cup	Grill-Roasted Garlic Barbecue Sauce (see recipe, page 47)	125 mL
¼ cup	sliced pitted black olives	60 mL
1 tbsp	extra-virgin olive oil	15 mL
1 tsp	Cajun Creole Seasoning and Rub (see recipe, page 17)	5 mL

FIRE-ROASTED SALSA

• Preheat grill to medium (350ºF/175ºC).

• Grill onion and tomatoes 7 to 10 minutes, or until tender and lightly charred (onion will take longer than tomatoes). Let cool before coarsely chopping.

• Combine chopped onions and tomatoes with the remaining ingredients and mix well. Set aside for at least 30 minutes to overnight for flavours to blend. Salsa will keep, covered, in refrigerator for 5 to 7 days.

Makes about 3½ cups
Prep Time: 20 minutes
Cook Time: 10 minutes

GRILLED STUFFED PORTOBELLOS

8	large portobello mushroom caps, soaked in very hot water for 30 minutes	8

MARINADE

¼ cup	olive oil	60 mL
¼ cup	cider vinegar	60 mL
1 tbsp	Garlic and Herb Rub (see recipe, page 26)	15 mL
1 cup	Grill-Roasted Garlic Barbecue Sauce (see recipe, page 47)	250 mL

STUFFING

2 cups	cooked BBQ chicken, shredded (such as from Beer-Can Chicken; see recipe, page 239)	500 mL
1	small onion, finely chopped	1
1½ cups	shredded Oka cheese	375 mL
½ cup	softened cream cheese	125 mL
¼ cup	Grill-Roasted Garlic Barbecue Sauce (see recipe, page 47)	60mL
1 tbsp	cider vinegar	15 mL
1 tbsp	chopped fresh sage	15 mL
	Salt and freshly ground black pepper	

TOPPING

½ cup	dry bread crumbs	125 mL
½ cup	freshly grated Parmesan cheese	125 mL

• Drain mushrooms and pat dry with paper towels.

MARINADE: Mix marinade ingredients and pour over mushrooms, turning to thoroughly coat. Allow to marinate for 1 hour.

STUFFING: In a bowl, stir together the chicken, onion, cheeses, BBQ sauce, vinegar, and sage. Season to taste with salt and pepper. Form the mixture into 8 balls and then flatten each to the size of the mushroom caps. Refrigerate until needed.

TOPPING: Combine the bread crumbs and Parmesan cheese in a small bowl and set aside.

• Preheat grill to medium-high (450°F/230°C).

• Place marinated mushrooms, gill side down, on a grill screen placed on the hot grill and cook for 4 to 5 minutes to lightly char and tenderize.

• Turn the grill down to medium (350°F/175°C), turn the mushrooms over, and top with the stuffing mixture. Top with a liberal dusting of the Parmesan/crumb mix.

• Close the lid and grill for 7 to 8 minutes more. The cheeses should be hot and bubbling and the crumbs golden.

• Remove from grill and serve as an appetizer or with a fresh garden salad as a unique main course.

Serves 8 as an appetizer, 4 as a main course.
Prep Time: 30 minutes
Marinade Time: 1 hour
Cook Time: 15 minutes

PLANKED BLUE CHEESE FIGS WRAPPED WITH PROSCIUTTO

untreated Napoleon® 12-inch cedar plank, soaked overnight

½ cup	crème de cassis liqueur	125 mL
1 tbsp	black peppercorns, cracked	15 mL
12	medium to large fresh black or green figs, halved lengthwise	12

FILLING

¾ cup	goat cheese, crumbled	175 mL
¾ cup	blue cheese, such as Gorgonzola or Roquefort, crumbled	175 mL
1	green onion, finely chopped	1
1 tbsp	fresh sage, finely chopped	15 mL
	Salt and freshly ground black pepper	
12	thin slices prosciutto	12
12	leaves Bibb lettuce	12
	Liquid honey to drizzle	

• Place crème de cassis in a large, flat, shallow dish. Sprinkle with the cracked peppercorns and then place the figs, cut side down, in the dish. Marinate for 20 minutes to 1 hour.

FILLING: While figs are marinating, mix cheeses, green onion, and sage. Season mixture with salt and pepper to taste.

• Preheat grill to medium-high (450°F/230°C).

• One at a time, remove the fig halves from the marinade. Place a heaping table-spoon (15 mL) of the cheese mixture on the cut side of a fig half. Place another fig half on the cheese. Press lightly together, then wrap the stuffed fig with a slice of prosciutto, pinching the prosciutto around the fig to hold it together.

• Set the stuffed figs on the presoaked plank and set the plank on the grill. Close the lid and grill-roast on the plank for about 5 to 6 minutes, or until heated through and the cheese starts to ooze.

• Place each stuffed fig on a lettuce leaf on a platter or on individual plates. Drizzle with honey and serve.

Serves 12
Prep Time: 30 minutes
Marinade Time: 1 hour
Cook Time: 5 minutes

TIP: Prepare the stuffed figs up to 8 hours ahead. Wrap and refrigerate until 30 minutes before grilling.

BACON-WRAPPED SCALLOPS

16	slices smoky bacon	16
16	large scallops (under 10 per lb/22 per kg)	16
2 tbsp	Seafood Seasoning and Rub (see recipe, page 22)	30 mL

• Partially cook the bacon, about 3 to 4 minutes a side, to render out most of the fat. Remove from the pan before the bacon begins to brown and pat dry with a paper towel. Set aside.

• Season scallops all over with the Seafood Seasoning and Rub, pressing the seasoning into the flesh. Wrap a slice of bacon around each scallop and secure with a toothpick.

• Place scallops on a wax paper–lined tray and refrigerate, covered, for 30 minutes.

• Preheat grill to medium-high (450ºF/230ºC).

• Grill scallops for 3 to 5 minutes a side, until they are lightly charred, just cooked through, and bacon is crisp.

• Serve immediately.

Serves 16 as an appetizer, 4 as a main course
Prep Time: 30 minutes
Cook Time: 10 minutes

RUMAKI SKEWERS:
MARINATED CHICKEN LIVERS, WATER CHESTNUTS, AND SMOKY BACON

24 large wooden skewers, soaked in water for at least 2 hours to overnight

DIP

½ cup	orange marmalade	125 mL
2 tbsp	raspberry vinegar	30 mL
2 tbsp	honey mustard	30 mL

MARINADE

¼ cup	raspberry vinegar	60 mL
¼ cup	chicken stock	60 mL
¼ cup	vegetable oil	60 mL
1	small onion, finely chopped	1
2	cloves garlic, minced	2
½ tsp	salt	2 mL
	Freshly ground black pepper, to taste	
12	chicken livers, cleaned and halved	12
12	canned water chestnuts, cut in half	12
12	slices smoky bacon, halved	12

DIP: Whisk together the marmalade, 2 tbsp (30 mL) vinegar, and honey mustard. Set aside.

MARINADE: Combine the ¼ cup (60 mL) vinegar, stock, oil, onion, garlic, salt, and pepper and whisk well to blend.

• Add chicken livers and water chestnuts and to the marinade and refrigerate, covered, for 1 to 2 hours.

• Remove livers and water chestnuts from marinade. Place marinade in a small saucepan and bring to a boil for 3 minutes. Set aside to baste the rumaki on the grill.

• Wrap a half slice of bacon around a piece of chicken liver and water chestnut. Secure each rumaki on the end of a presoaked toothpick or skewer.

• Preheat grill to medium (350ºF/175ºC).

• Grill skewers 4 to 5 minutes a side, basting liberally with the reserved boiled marinade, or until cooked through and bacon is crisp.

• Serve immediately with the orange marmalade dip on the side.

Makes 24 skewers. Serves 8 to 20 as part of an hors d'oeuvres service.
Prep Time: 30 minutes
Marinade Time: 2 hours
Cook Time: 10 minutes

TUMBLE BASKET BUFFALO WINGS
WITH BLUE CHEESE DIP

Napoleon® Tumble Basket

4 lbs	chicken wings, tips removed, halved at the joint	1.8 kg
¼ cup	Hot and Spicy Seasoning and Rub (see recipe, page 18)	60 mL

SAUCE

1 tbsp	vegetable oil	15 mL
1	small onion, finely diced	1
2–3	Scotch bonnet chiles, seeded and minced (optional)	2–3
2	green onions, thinly sliced	2
1	jar Napoleon® Buffalo Style Injector Seasoning	1
½ cup	liquid honey	125 mL
1 tbsp	Worcestershire sauce	15 mL
1 tbsp	fresh cilantro, chopped	15 mL
	Salt and freshly ground black pepper to taste	

- Rinse the wings in cold water and pat dry with paper towels. Place in a large bowl and add the Hot and Spicy Barbecue Seasoning and Rub. Using your hands, rub and toss the wings to coat evenly, massaging the spices well into the meat. Cover and refrigerate for 2 hours.

SAUCE: In a medium saucepan, heat the oil over medium heat. Sauté the onion, chiles (if using), and green onions for 3 to 5 minutes, until fragrant and tender. Add the Napoleon® Buffalo Style Injector Seasoning, honey, and Worcestershire sauce and bring to a boil. Reduce heat and simmer for 5 minutes, stirring once or twice. Remove from heat and stir in cilantro and salt and pepper to taste.

- Preheat grill to medium (350ºF/175ºC).

- Place wings in the Napoleon® Tumble Basket, attached to the rotisserie according to the manufacturer's instructions. Place a drip pan beneath the basket on the grill to catch drippings and prevent flare-ups as wings cook. Roast wings in basket for about 20 to 25 minutes, or until fully cooked, golden brown, and crisp. Whisk any drippings into the sauce.

- Carefully remove wings from the basket and toss with the sauce in a bowl.

- Serve with Chunky Blue Cheese Dip, celery and carrot sticks.

Serves 8 to 12 as an appetizer, 4 to 6 as a main course
Prep Time: 30 minutes
Marinade Time: 2 hours
Cook Time: 25 minutes

1 cup	mayonnaise	250 mL
1 cup	sour cream	250 mL
¼ cup	cold water	60 mL
2 tbsp	lemon juice	30 mL
1 cup	crumbled blue cheese	250 mL
2 tsp	Worcestershire sauce	10 mL
½ tsp	salt	2 mL
2	green onions, finely chopped	2
	Freshly ground black pepper to taste	

CHUNKY BLUE CHEESE DIP: In a large bowl, whisk together the mayonnaise, sour cream, water, and lemon juice.

- Stir in the blue cheese, Worcestershire sauce, salt, and green onions. Season to taste with pepper.

- Transfer to a sealed container and refrigerate until needed. Will keep up to a week.

Makes about 3½ cups (875 mL)
Prep Time: 20 minutes

PLANK-GRILLED POTATO SKINS

1 or 2 untreated Napoleon® 12-inch cedar planks, soaked overnight

6	baking potatoes	6
¼ cup	olive oil	60 mL
¼ cup	Memphis Rib Rub (see recipe, page 22)	60 mL
1 cup	Alabama White Barbecue Sauce (see recipe, page 43)	250 mL
8 slices	bacon, diced, fried crisp, and wrapped in paper towel	8
½ cup	shredded old orange cheddar cheese	125 mL
3–4	green onions, chopped	3–4

• Boil or bake potatoes until tender. Cut in half lengthwise and scoop out flesh (reserve for another use), leaving a ¼- to ½-inch (0.5 to 1 cm) shell.

• Preheat grill to medium-high (450°F/230°C).

• Cut each potato shell lengthwise into 3 to 5 wedges, depending on size of potato. Rub both sides of each wedge with olive oil. Sprinkle all over with Memphis Rib Rub.

• Place potato skins on the pre-soaked plank(s) and set plank(s) on the grill. Close lid and grill-roast for 10 to 12 minutes. Have a spray bottle of water handy in case plank catches fire.

• Open grill and generously brush wedges with the Alabama White Barbecue Sauce. Sprinkle with bacon and then with the cheese.

• Close the lid and grill a further 3 to 5 minutes, or until the cheese has melted and browned a bit and the edges of the potato skins are crispy.

• Remove from the grill and garnish with the chopped green onions. Serve immediately right from the plank (unless the plank is too burned) with more Alabama White Barbecue Sauce on the side.

TIP: These are equally as good off a Napoleon® Grill Topper or even straight on the grill, though you have to be very careful in that case.

Makes about 48 pieces. Serves 12 to 36 as part of an hors d'oeuvres service or 8 to 10 hungry guys at a tailgate party.
Prep Time: 1½ hours
Cook Time: 20 minutes

TIP: You can prepare the potato shells the day before you want to use them. You can also wrap them and freeze them for up to 3 weeks before making these.

GRILL-WOKKED MUSSELS
WITH LEMON AND HERBS

Napoleon® Round or Square Wok Topper

2 lbs	mussels, rinsed and cleaned of beards	1 kg
2 tbsp	olive oil	30 mL
1 tbsp	kosher salt	15 mL
2 tsp	freshly cracked pepper	10 mL
1 tbsp	fresh thyme, roughly chopped	15 mL
1 tbsp	fresh rosemary, roughly chopped	15 mL
3	cloves garlic, minced	3
2	lemons, halved	2
	Lemon wedges to serve	
¼ cup	unsalted butter, softened	60 mL

• Preheat grill to high (500ºF/260ºC).

• Set wok over grill to heat.

• In a large bowl, toss the mussels, oil, salt, pepper, thyme, rosemary, and garlic, to coat well.

• Carefully pour the seasoned mussels into the preheated wok. Close the grill and grill wok until the mussels open, about 7 to 10 minutes. Open grill about halfway through and squeeze the lemon halves over the mussels, close, and continue to cook.

• Carefully remove the wok and pour the mussels into serving bowls. Serve with the lemon wedges and top with a dollop of the soft butter.

• Serve with lots of toasted baguette and bottles of ice-cold beer.

Serves 4
Prep Time: 30 minutes
Cook Time: 10 minutes

SALADS

THAI CHILE AND LIME SLAW

4	green onions, thinly sliced on the diagonal	4
2	carrots, shredded	2
1	small green cabbage, thinly sliced	1
1	ripe mango, peeled, pitted, and diced	1
1	medium red onion, thinly sliced	1
2 cups	fresh pineapple, diced	500 mL
2	fresh limes, peeled, white removed, and coarsely chopped	2
2 tbsp	chopped fresh cilantro	30 mL

VINAIGRETTE

3	slices, ½-inch (1 cm) thick, fresh pineapple	3
¼ cup	spiced rum	60 mL
¼ cup	pineapple juice	60 mL
3 tbsp	freshly squeezed lime juice	45 mL
3 tbsp	liquid honey	45 mL
1–2	red chiles, seeded and minced	1–2
1	green onion, finely chopped	1
1 tbsp	finely chopped shallot	15 mL
2 tsp	peeled grated fresh ginger	10 mL
1 tbsp	chopped fresh cilantro, chopped	15 mL
½ cup	extra-virgin olive oil	125 mL
	Salt and freshly ground black pepper to taste	

• Combine the green onions, carrots, cabbage, mango, red onion, diced pineapple, limes, and cilantro in a large bowl. Mix well, cover, and refrigerate while making the vinaigrette.

VINAIGRETTE: Place the pineapple slices in a nonreactive bowl and pour the spiced rum over. Marinate for at least 1 hour.

• Preheat grill to medium-high (450°F/230°C).

• Reserving rum marinade, grill pineapple slices for 3 to 5 minutes per side. Remove pineapple slices from grill when lightly charred and tender. Cool slightly to handle and chop finely.

• Whisk together the pineapple, reserved rum, pineapple juice, lime juice, honey, chiles, green onion, shallot, ginger, and cilantro in a medium bowl. Whisk the oil into the mixture in a slow, steady stream to form a smooth emulsion. Season to taste with salt and pepper. Makes about 3 cups (750 mL) vinaigrette.

• Toss the cabbage mixture with 1 cup (250 mL) or more of the vinaigrette. Cover and refrigerate until ready to serve. Refrigerate leftover vinaigrette for up to 2 weeks.

Serves 6 to 8
Prep Time: 45 minutes
Marinade Time: 1 hour
Cook Time: 10 minutes

BAKED-POTATO SALAD
WITH MUSTARD AND OLIVES

6	medium Yukon gold potatoes	6
1	stalk celery, sliced	1
1	small red onion, diced	1
2	green onions, thinly sliced	2
2	eggs, hard-cooked and diced	2
12	green olives stuffed with pimentos, sliced	12
¾ cup	prepared creamy white salad dressing	175 mL
2 tbsp	prepared mustard	30 mL
	Salt and freshly ground black pepper to taste	

• Preheat grill or oven to medium-high (450°F/230°C).

• Place potatoes on the top shelf of the preheated grill, close lid, and grill-bake for 45 to 60 minutes, until just tender, or set potatoes directly on the upper rack of preheated oven and bake for 60 to 70 minutes, or until just tender.

• Allow baked potatoes to cool completely (4 to 6 hours to overnight in refrigerator).

• Cut the cold potatoes into bite-size chunks and place in a large bowl.

• Add the remaining ingredients and combine well. Season with salt and pepper.

• For best results, refrigerate overnight.

Serves 6 to 8
Prep Time: 1 hour to bake potatoes plus 30 minutes

CREAMY COLESLAW

½	medium green cabbage, very finely sliced	½
2	large carrots, grated	2
1	medium onion, finely chopped	1
3	green onions, thinly sliced on the diagonal	3
2 tbsp	granulated sugar	30 mL
1 tbsp	white vinegar	15 mL
½ tsp	salt	2 mL
½ cup	mayonnaise	125 mL
2 tsp	mustard powder	10 mL
1 tsp	freshly ground black pepper	5 mL
¼ tsp	cayenne pepper	1 mL

• Combine the cabbage, carrots, onion, green onions, sugar, vinegar, and salt in a nonreactive bowl and let marinate for 1 to 2 hours. Toss occasionally.

• Mix in the mayonnaise, mustard, black pepper, and cayenne.

• Refrigerate until ready to serve.

Serves 8
Prep Time: 45 minutes
Marinade Time: 2 hours

GRILLED HOT GERMAN POTATO SALAD

Napoleon® Multi-Grill Basket

2 tsp	salt	10 mL
2 lbs	new white potatoes, peeled, or scrubbed if leaving peel on	1 kg
¼ cup	olive oil	60 mL
	Salt and freshly ground black pepper to taste	
6	slices thick-sliced smoked bacon, cut in ¼-inch (0.5 cm) strips	6
1	medium red onion, halved lengthwise, lightly grilled, then thinly sliced	1
3 ribs	celery, finely diced	3
2 tbsp	fresh parsley, chopped	30 mL

DRESSING

2 tbsp	yellow or brown mustard seeds	30 mL
¼ cup	white wine vinegar	60 mL
½ cup	chicken broth, homemade or store-bought or made with good-quality base	125 mL

• Cut potatoes in even, large, bite-size pieces (halves, quarters, or eighths, depending on the size of the potatoes).

• In a large pot, bring 20 cups (5 L) of water to a boil. Add the salt and then the potatoes. Cook until just undercooked, about 7 to 9 minutes.

• While potatoes are cooking, line a baking sheet with lots of paper towel. Drain the potatoes when done and set on the paper towels to dry. Discard the paper towels and drizzle the potatoes with olive oil, salt, and pepper. Toss to coat thoroughly.

• Preheat the grill to medium-high (450ºF/230ºC).

• On your side burner, place a skillet over medium-high heat and fry the bacon until brown and crisp. Lift with a slotted spoon and set in a large bowl. Reserve the drippings.

• Place the oiled potatoes in the Napoleon® Multi-Grill Basket and set on the grill for about 4 minutes a side, or until lightly charred and soft to the bite.

• Add the grilled potatoes, onion, celery, and parsley to the bacon.

DRESSING: Meanwhile, soak the mustard seeds in the vinegar briefly (10 to 15 minutes) Bring the chicken stock to a boil; add the mustard mixture and 2 tbsp (30 mL) of the reserved bacon drippings.

• Pour over the potato salad and toss well to coat. Season with salt and pepper and serve while still warm.

Serves 6 to 8
Prep Time: 45 minutes
Cook Time: 8 to 10 minutes

GRILLED VEGETABLE SALAD
WITH GOAT CHEESE AND CHIPOTLE DRESSING

Napoleon® Multi-Grill Basket

1	large sweet yellow onion, sliced	1
2	zucchini, thinly sliced	1
8	large, mushrooms, quartered	8
2	red bell peppers, seeded and sliced	2
1	bunch asparagus, trimmed and cut into 2-inch (5 cm) pieces	1
1 tbsp	Cajun Creole Seasoning and Rub (see recipe, page 17)	15 mL
2 tbsp	olive oil	30 mL

SMOKED CHIPOTLE DRESSING

2–3	chipotle peppers (canned in adobo), puréed	2–3
½ cup	cider vinegar	125 mL
¼ cup	liquid honey	60 mL
2 tbsp	chopped fresh cilantro	30 mL
1 tsp	ground cumin	5 mL
1 tsp	salt	5 mL
	Juice of 2 limes	
¾ cup	olive oil	175 mL
1 tbsp	chopped fresh thyme	15 mL
½ cup	crumbled goat cheese	125 mL
	Salt and freshly ground black pepper	

• Place the onions, zucchini, mushrooms, peppers, and asparagus in a large bowl. Season with the Cajun Creole Seasoning and Rub and oil. Toss well to coat with the seasoning and oil. Place in a Napoleon® Multi-Grill Basket.

DRESSING: In a food processor, combine the pureed chipotles, vinegar, honey, cilantro, cumin, salt, and lime juice. Blend until smooth. With processor running, pour in the oil in a slow, steady stream to form a smooth emulsion. Pour into a bowl, cover, and refrigerate until needed.

• Preheat grill to medium-high (450ºF/230ºC).

• Grill vegetables in the basket for 8 to 10 minutes per side, until lightly charred and tender.

• Remove vegetables from the basket and place in a large bowl. Toss well with dressing, fresh thyme, and goat cheese.

• Season to taste with salt and pepper.

Serves 8
Prep Time: 45 minutes
Cook Time: 20 minutes

GRILLED FENNEL SALAD
WITH PANCETTA, ORANGES, AND RED ONIONS

2	fennel bulbs, root and stem trimmed and sliced lengthwise in 3 to 5 slices, ½ inch (1 cm) thick	2
1	medium red onion, halved	1
3 tbsp	extra-virgin olive oil	45 mL
3	green onions, thinly sliced on the diagonal	3
1	medium yellow banana pepper, finely diced	1
1	cubanelle pepper, julienned	1
2	large navel oranges, peeled and segmented	2
2 tbsp	fresh basil, chopped	30 mL

DRESSING

3 tbsp	olive oil	45 mL
3 tbsp	frozen orange juice concentrate, thawed	45 mL
3 tbsp	white wine vinegar	45 mL
4 tsp	mustard powder	20 mL
	Salt and freshly ground black pepper to taste	
8	slices pancetta	8
1 tbsp	fresh parsley, chopped	15 mL
1 tbsp	fresh thyme, chopped	15 mL
1 tsp	poppy seeds or black mustard seeds	10 mL

• Preheat grill to medium-high (450ºF/230ºC).

• Brush fennel and red onion with oil and grill for 3 to 5 minutes per side, or until lightly charred and tender. Remove from grill, cool slightly to handle, and slice thinly.

• In a large bowl, combine the grilled fennel and onion, green onions, banana pepper, cubanelle pepper, orange segments, and basil.

DRESSING: Whisk together the oil, orange juice concentrate, vinegar, and 2 tsp (10 mL) of the dry mustard in a small bowl. Season to taste with salt and pepper.

• Pour dressing over the fennel mixture and toss to coat. Cover and refrigerate for 1 hour.

• Fry the pancetta over medium-high heat for 1 to 2 minutes a side, or until crisp. Remove to paper towel and pat to remove excess oil. Thinly slice.

• Sprinkle pancetta, parsley, thyme, poppy seeds and remaining 2 tsp (10 mL) of dry mustard over the salad and toss well. Serve immediately.

Serves 6 to 8
Prep Time: 30 minutes
Marinade Time: 1 hour
Cook Time: 20 minutes

TIP: When grilling layered vegetables like fennel or onions, trim but do not remove the root end. If you leave the root on, it will hold the piece together on the grill. Remove it after you are finished grilling.

BAKED SWEET POTATO SALAD
WITH VANILLA-MAPLE VINAIGRETTE

4	large sweet potatoes	4
8	slices double-smoked bacon	8
1	medium red bell pepper, diced	1
⅔ cup	celery, diced	150 mL
4–5	green onions, thinly sliced on the diagonal	4–5
½ cup	beer nuts, lightly crushed	125 mL
1 tbsp	chopped fresh parsley	15 mL
1 tbsp	chopped fresh rosemary, chopped	15 mL
1 tbsp	chopped fresh thyme, chopped	15 mL

VANILLA-MAPLE VINAIGRETTE

1	vanilla bean, split in half and seeded, seeds reserved	1
2 tbsp	hot water	30 mL
3 tbsp	pure maple syrup	45 mL
3 tbsp	champagne vinegar or white wine vinegar	45 mL
1	shallot, finely chopped	1
1 tbsp	Dijon mustard	15 mL
3 tbsp	vegetable oil	45 mL

• Preheat grill to medium-high (450°F/230°C).

• Place sweet potatoes on the upper shelf of preheated grill and close lid. Roast for 45 to 60 minutes, or longer depending on size, until just cooked and tender but not mushy when pierced with a wooden skewer. Let cool slightly to handle, peel, and cut into bite-size pieces, 1 to 1½ inches (2.5 to 4 cm). Cool completely.

• Grill bacon slices until crispy, remove from grill, and dice in ½- to ¾-inch (1 to 2 cm) chunks.

• In a large bowl, combine sweet potato, bacon, red pepper, celery, green onions, beer nuts, parsley, rosemary, and thyme. Toss well and set aside.

VANILLA-MAPLE VINAIGRETTE: Place vanilla bean and seeds in a bowl with the hot water. Let sit 10 to 20 minutes.

• Whisk together the maple syrup, vinegar, shallot, and mustard. While continually whisking, drizzle in the oil to form an emulsion. Whisk in the vanilla mixture.

• Pour the vinaigrette over the sweet potato salad and mix well to coat. Serve immediately.

Serves 6 to 8
Prep Time: 1 hour to bake potatoes plus 45 minutes

TOMATO, BABY BOCCONCINI, AND GRILLED
BREAD SALAD WITH CUCUMBER, GRILLED PEPPERS, ONION, AND BLACK OLIVES

12	baby bocconcini	12
2	dill pickle, cucumbers, or half an English cucumber, cut in ½-inch (1 cm) chunks	2
1	red onion, halved, grilled (see page 54), and coarsely diced	1
1 large	large yellow or red bell pepper, grilled (see page 55) and coarsely diced	1
2 cups	grape tomatoes, grilled to char	500 mL
¾ cup	whole pitted black olives	175 mL
2 tbsp	Grill-Roasted Garlic (see page 56), mashed	30 mL
2 tbsp	chopped fresh herbs (such as basil, oregano, and parsley)	30 mL
3 tbsp	olive oil	45 mL
¼ cup	balsamic vinegar	60 mL
3 tbsp	liquid honey (or more to taste)	45 mL
	Salt and freshly ground black pepper	

GRILLED BREAD

1	loaf crusty white Italian bread	1
3 tbsp	balsamic vinegar	45 mL
¼ cup	extra-virgin olive oil	60 mL
3 tbsp	Grill-Roasted Garlic, mashed (see page 56)	45 mL
	Salt and freshly ground pepper	

• In a large bowl, combine the bocconcini, pickle, onions, bell pepper, tomatoes, olives, 2 tbsp (30 mL) Grill-Roasted Garlic, and herbs; toss well to mix.

• Drizzle olive oil, vinegar, and honey over the tomato mixture and toss to coat well. Season to taste with salt and black pepper.

• Marinate at room temperature for 1 hour, tossing occasionally.

GRILLED BREAD: Preheat grill to medium high (450ºF/230ºC).

• Slice the bread in half lengthwise.

• Whisk together the balsamic vinegar, oil, and 3 tbsp (45 mL) roasted garlic. Season to taste with salt and black pepper. Brush liberally on the cut sides of the bread and let marinate for 15 minutes.

• Grill the bread, cut side down first, until lightly browned and crisp all over. Cut the bread into 1-inch (2.5 cm) cubes.

• Toss the crisp bread cubes into the salad and mix well. Serve immediately.

Serves 6 to 8
Prep Time: 45 minutes
Marinade Time: 1 hour
Cook Time: 10 minutes

PASTA SALAD
WITH GRILLED SCALLOPS, ONIONS, AND PISTACHIOS

4 cups	rigatoni pasta, cooked al dente, cooled with cold water, and drained well	1 L
¼ cup	extra-virgin olive oil	60 mL

DRESSING

⅓ cup	Grill-Roasted Garlic (see recipe, page 56)	75 mL
3 tbsp	fresh basil, chopped	45 mL
½ cup	vegetable oil	125 mL
⅓ cup	white balsamic vinegar	75 mL
2 tbsp	freshly squeezed lemon juice	30 mL
	Salt and freshly ground black pepper	
24 large	sea scallops (about 2 lbs/1 kg)	24
3 tbsp	Seafood Seasoning and Rub (see recipe, page 22)	45 mL
6	large plum tomatoes, cut in half lengthwise	6
2	red onions, peeled and cut into wedges through the root end	2
3 tbsp	extra-virgin olive oil	45 mL
	Salt and freshly ground black pepper	
4	green onions, sliced in 1-inch (2.5 cm) pieces	4
⅓ cup	pistachios, coarsely crushed	75 mL
½ cup	shaved or coarsely grated fresh Parmesan cheese	125 mL

• Place drained pasta in a large bowl and toss with the ¼ cup (250 mL) olive oil to coat thoroughly.

DRESSING: Whisk together Grill-Roasted Garlic, basil, vegetable oil, vinegar, lemon juice, and salt and pepper and set aside.

• Preheat grill to medium-high (450ºF/230ºC).

• Rub the scallops with the Seafood Seasoning and Rub, pressing well into the scallops. Place on the preheated grill and cook for 2 to 3 minutes a side, or until just cooked through. Remove and let cool.

• Lower heat on grill to medium (350ºF/175ºC).

• Toss tomatoes and red onions in the 3 tbsp (45 mL) olive oil and season with salt and pepper to taste. Grill until lightly charred and tender, about 10 to 12 minutes. Let cool.

• Cut scallops into quarters or sixths depending on size. Chop tomatoes in large chunks and slice onions into ½-inch (1 cm) segments.

• Toss dressing, scallops, tomatoes, red onions, and green onions into the large bowl with the pasta and mix very well.

• Garnish with pistachios and Parmesan cheese.

Serves 6 to 8
Prep Time: 45 minutes
Cook Time: 20 minutes

PORTOBELLO MUSHROOM AND CIPOLLINI ONION SALAD

Napoleon® Multi–Grill Basket

8	large portobello mushroom caps	8
1 tsp	salt	5 mL
4 cups	hot water	1 L

MARINADE

½ cup	liquid honey	125 mL
½ cup	hoisin sauce	125 mL
¼ cup	soy sauce	60 mL
¼ cup	rice vinegar	60 mL
1 tbsp	freshly ground black pepper	15 mL
1 tbsp	fresh cilantro, chopped	15 mL
1 tbsp	sesame seeds	15 mL
1 tbsp	grainy mustard	15 mL
1 tsp	toasted sesame oil	5 mL
	Salt	
1½ cups	fresh cipollini onions, trimmed and peeled	375 mL
3 tbsp	vegetable oil	45 mL
	or	
1½ cups	cipollini onions in oil (available at Italian markets), drained	375 mL
4	bunches arugula	4
½ cup	goat cheese, crumbled	125 mL
1 tbsp	fresh cilantro, chopped	15 mL

• Brush the portobellos to remove any dirt. Place mushrooms in a large bowl. Dissolve salt in hot water and pour over the mushrooms. Place a plate over the mushrooms to fully submerge them, cover with plastic wrap, and let steep for 15 minutes.

MARINADE: Whisk together the honey, hoisin sauce, soy sauce, vinegar, pepper, cilantro, sesame seeds, mustard, and sesame oil. Season to taste with salt.

• Drain mushrooms and pat dry with paper towels. Place, gill side up, in a flat glass dish. Pour the marinade over the mushrooms and let marinate for 2 hours.

• Preheat the grill to medium-high (450°F/230°C).

• Remove mushrooms from the marinade, reserving the marinade for basting. If using fresh cipollini, toss them in the vegetable oil to coat. Secure the mushrooms and onions in the basket.

• Place the basket on the grill with the mushrooms gill side up. Grill until lightly charred and tender, about 4 to 5 minutes a side, basting frequently with the reserved marinade.

• Carefully remove the basket from the grill and empty. Allow the mushrooms and onions to cool slightly, then slice the mushroom caps into ¼-inch (0.5 cm) slices.

• Arrange the arugula on a platter. Toss the onions and mushroom slices together and arrange over the arugula. Top with goat cheese and cilantro.

Serves 6 to 8
Prep Time: 45 minutes
Marinade Time: 2 hours
Cook Time: 10 minutes

GRILLED ONION, BACON, AND ARTICHOKES ON WILTED GREENS

DRESSING

¾ cup	extra-virgin olive oil	175 mL
4	cloves garlic, minced	4
⅓ cup	cider vinegar	75 mL
2 tbsp	liquid honey	30 mL
2 tbsp	liquid honey	30 mL
2 tbsp	prepared mustard	30 mL
1 tbsp	cider vinegar	15 mL
8–10	slices double-smoked bacon	8–10
1	medium red onion, peeled and cut into wedges through the root end	1
1 tbsp	extra-virgin olive oil	15 mL
8	marinated artichokes (available at supermarkets)	8
12–16 cups	torn mixed lettuces (such as Bibb, iceberg, baby spinach)	3–4 L
1½ cups	grape tomatoes, halved if large	375 mL
	Sea salt and freshly ground black pepper to taste	

• Preheat grill to medium (350°F/175°C).

DRESSING: In a saucepan, slowly heat the olive oil, garlic, vinegar, and 2 tbsp (30 mL) honey over medium to low heat, just to below a simmer. Set aside but keep warm.

• In a small bowl, combine the 2 tbsp (30 mL) honey, prepared mustard, and cider vinegar.

• Place bacon slices on grill and brush with half of the honey-mustard glaze. Grill for 2 to 3 minutes, turn, brush with the remaining mixture, and grill until crisp on both sides, watching for flare-ups. Remove from grill and cut in ½- to ¾-inch (1 to 2 cm) chunks.

• Brush red onion wedges with the 1 tbsp (15 mL) olive oil and grill for 3 to 5 minutes each side, or until lightly charred and tender. Remove from grill, cool slightly to handle, and roughly chop.

• Remove artichokes from marinade and drain excess liquid. Slice in half lengthwise through the root end. Place on the grill and char lightly, about 2 to 3 minutes, turning frequently to prevent flare-ups.

• Place lettuces in a large serving bowl or on a platter. Pour the warm dressing over and toss lightly. Greens will diminish in volume by about half.

• Sprinkle the grilled bacon, onion, artichokes, and grape tomatoes over the wilted greens. Season with lots of pepper and salt. Serve immediately.

Serves 6 to 8
Prep Time: 45 minutes
Cook Time: 20 minutes

AVOCADO AND GRILLED PINEAPPLE SALAD

1	ripe pineapple, peeled, cored, and cut in ¾-inch (2 cm) slices	1
2	large navel oranges, peeled, white removed, and cut in ¾-inch (2 cm) slices	2
2 tbsp	extra-virgin olive oil	30 mL
1½ cups	chopped celery (about 2 stalks)	375 mL
3 cups	diced English cucumber	750 mL
½ cup	coarsely chopped fresh basil	125 mL
2	jalapeño peppers, seeded and minced	2

DRESSING

1⅓ cups	buttermilk	325 mL
¼ cup	freshly squeezed lime juice	60 mL
2 tbsp	extra-virgin olive oil	30 mL
1 tbsp	Grill-Roasted Garlic (see page 56)	15 mL
2½ tbsp	finely chopped fresh mint	37 mL
¼ cup	unsweetened shredded coconut	60 mL
2 tsp	sea salt	10 mL
1 tsp	freshly ground black pepper	5 mL
2½ cups	¾-inch (2 cm) cubed Haas avocado (about 2)	625 mL
	Whole lettuce leaves (such as Bibb, romaine, leaf, etc.)	

• Preheat grill to medium-high (450ºF/230ºC).

• Brush pineapple and orange slices with the 2 tbsp (30 mL) oil and place on the grill. Grill until lightly charred and pineapple is tender. Remove and cool. Chop into ¾-inch (2 cm) dice.

• In a large bowl, combine pineapple, orange, celery, cucumber, basil, and jalapeños.

DRESSING: Whisk together buttermilk, lime juice, and oil. Add Grill-Roasted Garlic, mint, coconut, salt, and pepper. Whisk well.

• Pour dressing over the pineapple-orange mixture and mix well. Gently fold in diced avocado.

• Arrange the salad over the lettuce leaves on a serving platter. Serve immediately.

Serves 6 to 8
Prep Time: 30 minutes
Cook Time: 10 minutes

THAI-STYLE GRILLED GREEK SALAD

1	medium English cucumber, cut in 1-inch (2.5 cm) cubes	1
1	small red onion, peeled, halved, grilled, and chopped coarsely	1
3	plum tomatoes, grilled and cut in 1-inch (2.5 cm) cubes	3
2	green onions, grilled and sliced on the diagonal into 1-inch (2.5 cm) pieces	2
2	celery stalks, sliced into 1-inch (2.5 cm) pieces	2
1	small green bell pepper, seeded, halved, grilled, and cut in 1-inch (2.5 cm) pieces	1

DRESSING

1–3	red chiles, seeded and finely chopped	1–3
2	cloves garlic, minced	2
¼ cup	olive oil	60 mL
2 tbsp	freshly squeezed lime juice	30 mL
3 tbsp	rice vinegar	45 mL
1 tbsp	granulated sugar	15 mL
2 tbsp	chopped fresh mint	30 mL
1 tbsp	fresh cilantro, chopped	15 mL
	Salt and freshly ground black pepper to taste	
½ cup	crumbled feta cheese (optional)	125 mL

• In a large bowl, combine the cucumbers, red onion, tomatoes, green onions, celery, and green pepper.

DRESSING: In a small saucepan, combine the chiles, garlic, oil, lime juice, vinegar, and sugar. Bring just to a low boil, stirring frequently. Remove from heat and let cool for 5 minutes.

• Pour dressing over the cucumber mixture and stir to mix. Let cool completely.

• Stir in the mint and cilantro. Season to taste with salt and pepper and serve.

• Garnish with the crumbled feta if you like!

Serves 6 to 8
Prep Time: 45 minutes
Cook Time: 5 minutes

GRILLED CAESAR SALAD

CROUTONS

½ cup	melted butter	125 mL
½ cup	extra-virgin olive oil	125 mL
2 tbsp	puréed garlic	15 mL
2	large baguettes, sliced in half lengthwise	2
3–4	medium heads romaine lettuce, washed, dark outer leaves discarded	3–4
2 tbsp	extra-virgin olive oil	30 mL

DRESSING

4	eggs	4
6	anchovy fillets, minced	6
1 tbsp	minced garlic	15 mL
2 tbsp	Dijon mustard	30 mL
¼ cup	freshly squeezed lemon juice	60 mL
1 cup	extra-virgin olive oil	250 mL
	Salt and freshly ground black pepper to taste	
½ cup	freshly ground Parmesan cheese	125 mL

• Preheat grill to medium-high (450ºF/230ºC).

CROUTONS: Whisk together the butter, ½ cup (125 mL) oil, and garlic. Slice the bread in half lengthwise. Brush the garlic butter liberally on all sides of the bread. Grill the bread, cut side down first, until lightly browned and crisp all over. Cut the bread into 1-inch (2.5 cm) cubes.

• Brush romaine with the 2 tbsp (30 mL) oil and place on the grill. Cook just until outer leaves are marked and romaine is slightly wilted (about 5 minutes). Tear leaves into large pieces and place in a large bowl.

DRESSING: Bring a small pot of water to a rolling boil. Gently lower the eggs into the water and boil a scant 1 minute. Remove immediately to cold water to cool. Crack the eggs and separate the yolks to a medium bowl. Discard the whites.

• Add anchovy, garlic, Dijon, and lemon juice to the yolks to thoroughly combine.

• Whisk the 1 cup (250 mL) extra-virgin olive oil slowly into the yolk mixture, whisking constantly, to form an emulsion. Season with salt and pepper. Add more lemon juice to taste if desired.

• Add about half the croutons and half the Parmesan cheese to the torn romaine. Add dressing to taste and mix well. Garnish with more croutons and cheese. Serve immediately.

Serves 6 to 8
Prep Time: 30 minutes
Cook Time: 10 minutes

SANDWICHES

THE GREAT CANADIAN BURGER, WITH PEAMEAL
BACON, OLD WHITE CHEDDAR, LETTUCE, TOMATO, ONION, AND PICKLES

3 lbs	regular ground beef	1.5 kg
¼ cup	butter, softened	60 mL
1	onion, finely chopped	1
3	cloves garlic, minced	3
1 tbsp	chopped fresh parsley	15 mL
1 tbsp	Worcestershire sauce	15 mL
1 tbsp	Dijon mustard	15 mL
to taste	Steak Spice (see recipe, page 18)	to taste
¾ lb	peameal bacon, sliced	375 g
¾ lb	old white cheddar cheese, sliced	375 g
6 or 12	burger buns (double burgers optional)	6 or 12
½ cup	melted butter for brushing buns	125 mL
2	beefsteak tomatoes, sliced	2
1	sweet onion, thinly sliced	1
4	dill pickles, sliced	4
1	head iceberg lettuce, separated into leaves	1

TIP: To really make these delicious burgers pop, try glazing them with Texas-Style Barbecue Sauce (see recipe, page 40) before topping with bacon and cheese.

• Preheat grill to medium-high (450ºF/230ºC).

• In a large bowl, mix together the beef, butter, onion, garlic, parsley, Worcestershire sauce, and mustard. Season to taste with Steak Spice.

• Form into twelve 4-oz (125 g) patties as uniform in size and thickness as possible. Grill burgers for 4 to 5 minutes per side for medium-well.

• Grill peameal slices for 1 to 2 minutes a side, or until juicy and warmed through. Place a slice on a burger patty and top with a slice of cheddar. Close lid for 1 to 2 minutes, or until cheese begins to melt.

• Brush cut side of burger buns with melted butter and grill, buttered side down, until crisp and golden brown.

• Place the cheese-and-bacon-topped patty on a bun bottom. Top with tomato, onion, and pickle slices. Place a lettuce leaf on top and serve immediately, open face, on a plate. Provide your favourite condiments, such as ketchup, mayonnaise, relish, mustard, etc.

Serves 6 or 12
Prep Time: 45 minutes
Cook Time: 15 minutes

BURGER TIPS

• All ground meats should be kept as cold as possible. Handle only as much as necessary to form your patty. Excessive massaging and kneading will only melt natural fats and increase the bacteria load.

• Patties should be as uniform in size and thickness as possible. If thickness is uneven and the patty is ball-like, the burgers will burn around the edges before the centres are properly cooked.

• Patties should be patted lightly (as you form them) to collapse air pockets where fat and fluids will gather and cause the burger to fall apart.

• Once the patties are formed, chilling them for an hour or more in the refrigerator will allow the meat to relax and the fat to solidify after handling.

• Do not use a spatula to press down on the patty as it cooks. This action does not speed up the cooking time. It only forces out the juices that hold all the flavour, leaving you with a flat, dry, tasteless piece of meat.

• The leaner the meat, the dryer the burger. Burgers by their nature are not meant to be lean. The best beef is freshly ground chuck with 15% to 20% fat, or use a good-quality regular ground beef for your beef burgers. For chicken and turkey, freshly ground thigh meat stays juiciest. For lamb and pork, ground shoulder is preferable.

• In all cases, freshly ground meat should be cooked and served within 24 hours of purchase.

• Keep a spray bottle of water by the grill to douse flare-ups from dripping fat.

• A cooked burger should be served and eaten straight from the grill. Precooking and reheating takes you straight back to dry and flavourless.

BURGER GARNISH 101

KETCHUP

MUSTARD — prepared yellow, Dijon, Pommery, honey, brown, etc.

RELISH — old-fashioned green, tomato, corn, Branston, piccalilli, or any that strikes your fancy

PICKLES — dill, bread and butter, kosher style with garlic, etc.

ONIONS — red, white, sweet, green; raw, grilled, pickled, fried, etc.

TOMATOES — beefsteak, plum, heirloom; fried green (make sure they are fresh)

PEPPERS — roasted red bell, jalapeño, pickled banana, etc.

SAUERKRAUT

CHEESE —There are no rules; cheddar to brie to Stilton

BACON — side, back, peameal; grilled, fried, etc.

FRIED EGG — very French, very good

MUSHROOMS — cremini, oyster, portobello, plain old field; grilled or fried

AVOCADO

PEANUT BUTTER — Do you eat peanut sauce on satay? So why not peanut butter on a burger? Try it. Especially with bacon.

LETTUCE — all kinds, but crisp varieties are best

GRILLED VEGETABLES — see page 54. They all work, slice thinly.

ROASTED GARLIC — mashed and spread on the bun

DRESSING — mayonnaise, blue cheese, ranch, Caesar, etc.

STEAK SAUCE — or any favoured barbecue sauce or hot sauce

CHILI — or smoked pulled pork (see page 236)

ONION RINGS — fried and breaded

And so on. Let your imagination lead.

CHICKEN BURGERS

2 lbs	ground chicken, thigh meat if possible	1 kg
3	boneless skinless chicken breasts (about 1 lb/450 g total), finely diced	3
1	small red onion, finely diced	1
2	cloves garlic, minced	2
1	jalapeño pepper, seeded and finely chopped	1
1¼ cups	Gourmet-Style Barbecue Sauce (see recipe, page 44), divided	300 mL
¼ cup	coarse fresh bread crumbs	60 mL
1½ tbsp	*The* Burger Seasoning! (see recipe, page 25)	22 mL
	Vegetable oil	
6–12	burger buns	6–12
	Burger garnish of your choice	

• Combine the ground and diced chicken with the onion, garlic, jalapeño, ¼ cup of the Gourmet-Style Barbecue Sauce, the bread crumbs, and the seasoning. Mix well, cover, and chill for at least 2 hours in the refrigerator.

• Form into 12 equal-sized patties as uniform in size and thickness as possible.

• Preheat grill to medium-high (450ºF/230ºC).

• Brush burgers with oil. Grill for 4 to 5 minutes per side, or until juices run clear and burger is well done (an instant-read meat thermometer should show an internal temperature of 165ºF/74ºC). Brush remaining barbecue sauce on the burgers as they grill.

• Grill buns, cut side down, to toast.

• Place burgers on the buns and serve immediately with your favourite garnishes.

Serves 6 to 12
Prep Time: 45 minutes
Cook Time: 15 minutes

PLANKED SALMON BURGER
WITH LEMON-DILL MAYO, PANCETTA, AND CUCUMBER PICKLE

untreated Napoleon® cedar plank, soaked for 2 to 24 hours

2 lbs	fresh salmon fillet, skinned and boned	1 kg
3	cloves garlic, minced	3
2	green onions, finely chopped	2
1 tbsp	Dijon mustard	15 mL
½ cup	panko crumbs (Japanese coarse bread crumbs)	125 mL
2 tsp	Seafood Seasoning and Rub (see recipe, page 22)	10 mL
1 tbsp	freshly squeezed lemon juice	15 mL
1	egg white	1
1 tbsp	fresh dill, chopped	15 mL

LEMON-DILL MAYO

1 cup	mayonnaise	250 mL
	Zest and juice of 1 lemon	
1 tbsp	fresh dill, chopped	15 mL
	Freshly ground black pepper	

CUCUMBER PICKLE

1	English cucumber, sliced thinly	1
1	medium red onion, sliced thinly	1
¼ cup	white vinegar	60 mL
1 tsp	kosher salt	5 mL
1 tsp	granulated sugar	5 mL
	Vegetable oil	
	Salt and freshly ground black pepper	
8	slices pancetta	8
8	fresh onion buns	8
8	leaves green leaf lettuce	8

• Roughly chop the salmon into 1-inch (2.5 cm) pieces. Place in the bowl of a food processor and pulse just until coarsely chopped and the salmon begins to bind together. Transfer to a bowl.

• Add garlic, onions, mustard, panko, Seafood Seasoning and Rub, lemon juice, egg white, and the 1 tbsp (15 mL) dill to the bowl and mix well. Form into 8 equal-sized patties as uniform in size and thickness as possible. Cover and refrigerate for 2 hours to chill and set the burgers.

LEMON-DILL MAYO: Combine mayonnaise, lemon zest and juice, the 1 tbsp (15 mL) dill, and pepper in a small bowl and mix well. Cover and refrigerate until needed.

CUCUMBER PICKLE: Place cucumber and onion in a medium-sized nonreactive bowl. In a small saucepan, combine vinegar, salt, and sugar and bring just to a simmer. Stir to dissolve salt and sugar, and pour over cucumber mixture. Toss to coat well, cover, and set aside to cool.

• Preheat grill to medium-high (450ºF/230ºC).

• Brush burgers with oil and season with salt and pepper. Arrange on the soaked plank. Place plank on the preheated grill, close the lid, and grill-roast for about 15 to 18 minutes, until medium-well (an instant-read meat thermometer should show an internal temperature of 165ºF/74ºC).

• Grill pancetta for 1 minute on each side.

• Grill buns, cut side down, to toast.

• Place lettuce leaves on the bun bottoms. Place burgers on lettuce, top with 1 tbsp (15 mL) of the lemon-dill mayonnaise, then with some cucumber pickle. Finish with a slice of pancetta and top with the bun top. Serve immediately.

Serves 8
Prep Time: 1 hour
Cook Time: 25 minutes

TIP: Don't rush your food. If you try to flip a burger or a piece of meat or, especially, a piece of fish, and it doesn't yield easily, it is either not ready to flip or the grill wasn't preheated. Step back and take a breath. It will yield to the spatula easily when it's ready. This is not a race.

BACON-WRAPPED PORK BURGERS
WITH RED CABBAGE SLAW

2 lbs	lean ground pork	1 kg
8 oz	Asiago cheese, cut in ½ inch (1 cm) cubes	250 g
1	medium onion, peeled and sliced lengthwise through the root	1
1	medium red bell pepper, seeded and cut in chunks	1
2 tbsp	olive oil	30 mL
1 tbsp	Hot and Spicy BBQ Seasoning and Rub (see recipe, page 18)	15 mL
4	green onions, thinly sliced	4
1 tbsp	*The* Burger Seasoning! (see recipe, page 25)	15 mL
16	slices streaky bacon	16
½ cup	Italian Marinade (see recipe, page 36)	125 mL
8	fresh Italian ciabatta buns	8

• Place 1 lb (500 g) of pork in food processor. Process meat to a smooth texture. Turn meat out into a large bowl and add the other 1 lb of ground pork. Mix lightly, cover, and refrigerate until needed.

• Place diced cheese in the freezer for at least 20 minutes.

• Preheat grill to medium-high (450ºF/230ºC).

• Brush onions and peppers with olive oil and season with Hot and Spicy BBQ Seasoning and Rub. Grill until lightly charred and tender. Remove and let cool slightly. Dice and set aside to cool.

• Add completely cooled onions and peppers, green onions, and Burger Seasoning to the pork mixture and mix well to fully incorporate ingredients.

• Add frozen cheese to the burger mixture and mix. Form into 8 equal-sized patties as uniform in size and thickness (about ¼ inch/1 cm thick) as possible. Wrap 2 slices of streaky bacon around each patty, like a parcel, and secure with a toothpick.

• Place patties in the refrigerator for 2 hours to chill and set.

• Preheat grill to medium (350ºF/175ºC).

• Grill, basting with the Italian Marinade, until patty is fully cooked, bacon is crisp, and cheese is melting and soft, about 5 to 6 minutes a side.

• Slice the ciabatta buns in half and grill, cut sides down, until golden brown.

• Place burgers on a bun and serve with Red Cabbage Slaw, your favourite garnishes, and more marinade on the side for dipping.

Serves 8
Prep Time: 45 minutes
Cook Time: 15 minutes

¼ cup	olive oil	60 mL
4 cups	shredded red cabbage	1 L
2	large Gala apples, peeled, cored and thinly sliced	2
1	small red onion, peeled, halved and thinly sliced	1
2 tbsp	liquid honey	30 mL
2 tbsp	red wine vinegar	30 mL
1 tsp	ground caraway seed	5 mL
	Salt and freshly ground black pepper to taste	

RED CABBAGE SLAW: Preheat a large skillet on medium-high heat and add the oil. Add the cabbage, apples, and onions and sauté, stirring occasionally, for about 6 to 8 minutes, or until the slaw has just begun to soften.

• Add the honey, vinegar, and caraway, and stir well to combine. Remove from heat and let cool.

• Season with salt and pepper and serve. Especially good on or beside pork.

Serves 6 to 8
Prep Time: 30 minutes
Cook Time: 15 minutes

CILANTRO-AND-LIME-MARINATED CHICKEN AND STEAK FAJITAS WITH GUACAMOLE AND PAPAYA SALSA

Napoleon® Multi-Grill Basket

| 2 lbs | flank steak | 1 kg |
| 2 lbs | boneless skinless chicken breasts (about 6) | 1 kg |

MARINADE

2 cups	chopped cilantro	500 mL
1½ cups	olive oil	375 mL
6–8	cloves garlic, minced	6–8
½ cup	freshly squeezed lime juice	125 mL
	Zest of 3 limes, finely chopped	
1 tbsp	ground cumin	15 mL
2 tsp	ancho chile powder	10 mL
1 cup	olive oil	250 mL
1 tbsp	Grill-Roasted Garlic (see recipe, page 56), mashed	15 mL
3	large cubanelle peppers, seeded and cut into ½ inch (1 cm) strips	3
3	large bell peppers, red, yellow, and green, seeded and cut in ¾-inch (2 cm) strips	3
2	large red onions, peeled and halved lengthwise through the root	2
6–8	large brown field mushrooms, brushed clean	6–8
16–18	8-inch (10 cm) flour tortillas	16–18
	Guacamole (recipe follows)	
	Papaya Salsa (recipe follows)	
2 cups	sour cream	500 mL
5–6	green onions, sliced thinly on the diagonal	5–6
2	large beefsteak tomatoes, finely diced	2
3–4	chiles, such as jalapeño or serrano, seeded and chopped	3–4
	Freshly ground black pepper	

TIP: Nothing about fajitas is difficult, but they can be time consuming. To prevent constantly running back and forth to the kitchen, be organized. Do all the preparations ahead of time and arrange around the grill.

Use your multi-basket or the stainless steel griddle for the vegetables so you aren't fiddling with dozens of pieces of pepper, mushroom, and onion falling between the grill slats and otherwise escaping the fajita.

• Place the chicken breasts in a 13- by 9-inch (3 L) glass baking dish. Place the steak in another glass baking dish.

MARINADE: In a small bowl, whisk together the cilantro, 1½ cups (375 mL) oil, garlic, lime juice, lime zest, cumin, and ancho chile powder.

• Pour one-third of the marinade over the beef, cover, and refrigerate for 1 hour to overnight. Pour one-third of the marinade over the chicken, cover, and refrigerate for 1 to 2 hours. Turn the meats occasionally to coat well with the marinade. Reserve the remaining one-third of the marinade for later.

NOTE: Do not leave the chicken in the marinade for longer than 2 hours, or the lime juice will change the meat's texture.

• Preheat grill to medium-high (450°F/230°C).

• In a small bowl, whisk together the 1 cup (250 mL) olive oil and the Grill-Roasted Garlic. Place the cubanelles, bell peppers, onions, and mushrooms in a large bowl and toss with the garlic/olive oil mixture to coat. Secure in a multi-grill basket.

• Remove the chicken and steak from the marinades and drain. Discard the marinades.

• Stack tortillas in piles of 6 and wrap loosely with foil. Place on the back upper shelf of the grill to warm while cooking the meat and vegetables.

• Grill the chicken breasts until cooked through, about 6 to 7 minutes a side. Remove to a clean cutting board. Slice the breasts crosswise into thin strips, place on one half of a large serving platter, and drizzle with half of the reserved marinade.

• Grill the steak medium-rare, about 3 to 4 minutes a side. Remove to a clean cutting board and let stand for 10 minutes before slicing thinly across the grain on the diagonal. Place on the other half of the serving platter and drizzle with the rest of reserved marinade. Keep warm while finishing vegetables.

• Place the grill basket on the grill for 3 to 4 minutes a side, or until the vegetables

are slightly charred and softened. Remove from the basket and arrange on a platter.

• Place the platters of meat and vegetables on the table with the warm tortillas. Place bowls of Guacamole, Papaya Salsa, sour cream, green onions, tomatoes, chiles, and black pepper around the platters.

• To assemble, place some guacamole on the tortilla, top with chicken or steak, add some of the grilled veggies, and some salsa. Add any other of the condiments that appeal and roll the tortilla to enclose. Bon appétit!

Serves 8 to 12
Prep Time: 1 hour
Marinating Time: 2 hours and overnight
Cook Time: 45 minutes

2	avocados, peeled and seeded	2
3 tbsp	freshly squeezed lemon juice	45 mL
1 tbsp	fresh cilantro, chopped	15 mL
½	small red onion, diced	½
2	cloves garlic, minced	2
	Hot pepper sauce	
	Salt and freshly ground black pepper	

GUACAMOLE: In a bowl, mash the avocados well (though some chunks are desirable). Stir in the lemon juice, cilantro, onion, and garlic. Season to taste with the hot sauce, salt, and pepper. Cover and refrigerate until needed.

Makes about 2 cups (500 mL)
Prep Time: 20 minutes

1	ripe papaya, peeled, seeded, and finely diced	1
1	small red onion, finely diced	1
1	red bell pepper, seeded and finely diced	1
2	green onions, finely chopped	2
1	jalapeno pepper, seeded and diced finely	1
2 tbsp	freshly squeezed lime juice	30 mL
1 tbsp	fresh cilantro, chopped	15 mL
1 tbsp	olive oil	15 mL
2 tsp	fresh mint, chopped	10 mL
	Salt and freshly ground pepper	

PAPAYA SALSA: Combine all the ingredients and mix well. Cover and refrigerate until needed.

Makes about 2½ cups (625 mL)
Prep Time: 45 minutes

TIP: Cross-contamination. An ugly term. Never put cooked meat on anything but a clean surface. Raw and cooked meats must never ever meet. Food poisoning is often caused by carelessness. Don't send your guests home with that type of souvenir.

OLD-FASHIONED, REALLY GRILLED, HAM AND CHEESE

Napoleon® Multi-Grill Basket

¼ cup	butter	60 mL
16	slices Texas toast or thick-sliced white sandwich bread	16
16	thick (or double up) slices processed cheese	16
24	slices Black Forest ham, in loose rolls	24
	Salt and freshly ground black pepper	

• Preheat grill to medium (350ºF/175ºC).

• Generously butter one side of each slice of bread. Place 8 slices butter side down.

• Lay 1 slice of processed cheese on each piece of bread, top with 2 rolls of ham, then another slice of cheese. Top with the remaining bread slices, butter side up.

• Secure the sandwiches snugly in the multi-grill basket. Grill for 4 to 5 minutes a side, turning frequently to prevent burning. Grill until the sandwiches are golden brown and crisp, and cheese is melted.

• Slice on the diagonal and season with salt and pepper. Serve with your favourite mustard or hot sauce on the side.

Serves 4 to 8
Prep Time: 20 minutes
Cook Time: 10 minutes

TIP: Great tailgating food. Set them up the night before, wrap and refrigerate. Grill any where you can set up the "Q."

GRILLED GROUPER BLT
WITH TRUE TARTAR SAUCE

MARINADE

1 tbsp	olive oil	15 mL
1	red onion, finely diced	1
4	cloves garlic, minced	4
2 tbsp	fresh thyme, chopped	30 mL
½ cup	Gourmet-Style Barbecue Sauce (see recipe, page 44)	125 mL
¼ cup	steak sauce	60 mL
2 tbsp	freshly squeezed lemon juice	30 mL
	Salt and freshly ground black pepper	
6	grouper fillets, skinless, each 4–5 oz (125–150 g), 1 inch (2.5 cm) thick	6
3 tbsp	Seafood Seasoning and Rub (see recipe, page 22)	45 mL
12	slices double-smoked bacon	12
12	slices sourdough bread, buttered	12
6	leaves green leaf lettuce	6
1–2	beefsteak tomatoes, sliced	1–2
	Tartar Sauce (recipe follows)	

MARINADE: In a medium saucepan, heat the oil over medium-high heat. Sauté the onion and garlic for 2 to 3 minutes, or until tender. Add thyme and green onions and cook for 1 minute more, stirring continuously. Add the Gourmet-Style Barbecue Sauce, steak sauce, and lemon juice. Bring to a boil, then reduce heat and simmer for 10 to 15 minutes, stirring occasionally. Season with salt and pepper to taste and pour into a glass dish. Cool completely.

• Season the fillets with Seafood Seasoning and Rub, massaging well into the flesh. Set in the marinade and turn to coat well. Marinate at room temperature for 45 to 60 minutes.

• Preheat grill to medium-high (450ºF/230ºC).

• Remove fillets from the marinade, reserving the marinade. Grill for 5 to 6 minutes a side, or until the fillets are just cooked through and flake easily, basting liberally with the marinade while cooking. Discard marinade when fish is done.

• Grill bacon slices until crispy.

• Place bread slices on the grill, buttered side down first. Grill to golden brown and crisp.

• Place 6 slices of toast buttered side up and set lettuce leaves on them. Top with the grouper fillets, the bacon, and then the tomato. Liberally spread Tartar Sauce on the buttered side of the remaining slices of toast and top the sandwiches. Serve immediately with more Tartar Sauce on the side.

Serves 4 to 6
Prep Time: 45 minutes
Marinade Time: 1 hour
Cook Time: 30 minutes

2	dill pickles, finely chopped	2
2	small shallots, finely chopped	2
2	green onions, finely chopped	2
2 cups	mayonnaise	500 mL
4 tbsp	capers, chopped	60 mL
2 tbsp	freshly squeezed lemon juice	30 mL
	Cayenne pepper	
	Salt and freshly ground black pepper	

TRUE TARTAR SAUCE: Combine the ingredients in a small bowl and mix well. Cover and refrigerate until needed.

Makes about 2 cups (500 mL)
Prep Time: 20 minutes

GRILLED CHEESE STEAK SANDWICH

4	beef tenderloin filets, each 6 oz (175 g)	4
2 tbsp	Steak Spice (see recipe, page 18)	30 mL
2 tbsp	butter	30 mL
6	cloves garlic, minced	6
1	medium onion, diced	1
2 cups	regular white mushrooms, sliced	500 mL
1 tbsp	fresh thyme, chopped	15 mL
1 tbsp	Dijon mustard	15 mL
	Salt and freshly ground black pepper	
8	slices brie	8
4	slices baguette, cut on the diagonal, about 4 inches (10 cm) long	4
1	bunch arugula	1

• Season beef with Steak Spice, massaging well into the meat. Cover and set aside.

• Preheat a sauté pan over medium-high heat on the side burner of the grill and melt the butter. Sauté the garlic and onions for 2 to 3 minutes and then add the mushrooms. Sauté for 10 to 15 minutes, stirring frequently, until the liquid has all evaporated and the mushrooms are tender and browned.

• Preheat grill to medium-high (450ºF/230ºC).

• Grill steaks for 2 to 3 minutes a side for medium rare.

• Top each steak with a quarter of the mushroom mixture and 2 slices of Brie. Close the lid and grill until the cheese starts to melt, 1 to 2 minutes.

• Lightly toast the baguette slices, cut side down. Top with arugula and then the cheese steak.

Serves 4
Prep Time: 20 minutes
Cook Time: 20 minutes

MEATBALL SUB
WITH FIRE-ROASTED TOMATO SALSA

Napoleon® Grill Topper

1 tbsp	olive oil	15 mL
1	onion, finely diced	1
4	cloves garlic, minced	4
6	slices pancetta, grilled crisp, cooled, and chopped	6
2 lbs	lean ground beef	1 kg
2	large eggs	2
½ cup	freshly grated Parmesan cheese	125 mL
¼ cup	finely chopped fresh curly parsley	60 mL
½ cup	white bread crumbs, preferably fresh	125 mL
	Salt and freshly ground black pepper	
¼ cup	olive oil	60 mL

FIRE-ROASTED TOMATO SALSA

8	ripe plum tomatoes, halved	8
2	medium red onions, peeled and thickly sliced	2
¼ cup + 3 tbsp	olive oil	60 mL +45 mL
	Salt and freshly ground pepper to taste	
2 tbsp	chopped fresh curly parsley	30 mL
2 tbsp	chopped fresh basil	30 mL
3 tbsp	Grill-Roasted Garlic (see recipe, page 56)	45 mL
2 tbsp	balsamic vinegar	30 mL
1 cup	Grill-Roasted Garlic Barbecue Sauce (see recipe, page 47)	250 mL
½ cup	sliced black olives	125 mL
	Salt and freshly ground black pepper	
3	fresh baguettes, 16–18 inches (28–30 cm) long, sliced in half lengthwise	3
1 cup	olive oil	250 mL
	leaf lettuce leaves	
1 lb	provolone cheese, sliced	500 g

• Sauté the onions and minced garlic in olive oil for 2 to 3 minutes, or until tender and fragrant. Cool.

• Combine onion mixture, pancetta, ground beef, eggs, Parmesan, parsley, bread crumbs, and salt and pepper in a large bowl. Mix well, cover, and chill for 1 to 2 hours.

• Form meat mixture into tight compact balls about the size of large walnuts, or larger if preferred. Chill for 1 hour.

• Preheat grill to medium (350ºF/175ºC).

• Brush the ¼ cup (60 mL) oil in the Napoleon® Grill Topper and fill with the meatballs in a single layer, taking care not to crowd too tightly. Grill-roast until cooked through, about 15 to 17 minutes. Chill.

NOTE: Can be frozen until needed at this point.

FIRE-ROASTED TOMATO SALSA: Toss the tomatoes and red onion in the ¼ cup (60 mL) oil and season with salt and pepper. Grill until lightly charred and tender, 7 to 10 minutes (tomatoes will be done sooner than the onions). Chop tomatoes and onions. In a bowl, combine with the 3 tbsp (45 mL) olive oil, parsley, basil, Grill-Roasted Garlic, balsamic vinegar, Fire-Roasted Barbecue Sauce, and olives. Mix well, taking care not to crush the tomatoes to pulp. Season to taste with salt and pepper. Set aside. Salsa will keep 3 weeks refrigerated.

• Brush cut sides of baguettes with the 1 cup (250 mL) olive oil. Grill baguettes for 1 to 2 minutes a side, or until lightly browned and crisp. Place lettuce leaves on the cut side of the bottom of baguettes. Place meatballs on the lettuce and top with provolone slices. Apply liberal spoonfuls of the salsa and place the tops on the baguettes, pressing down for a few seconds to allow filling to set in the bread.

• Cut the baguettes into 2, 3, or 4 pieces as desired and serve immediately with more salsa on the side.

Makes 3 large submarines to serve 6 to 8 or more
Prep Time: Meatballs — 45 minutes plus chill times; Salsa — 30 minutes
Cook Time: Meatballs — 20 minutes; Salsa — 10 minutes

GRILLED PORTOBELLO STACKS

12	portobello mushroom caps	12
	Very hot water	
	balsamic vinegar	
4	cloves garlic, minced	4
1 tbsp	Steak Spice (see recipe, page 18)	15 mL
¼ cup	olive oil plus more for drizzling	60 mL
2–3	ripe tomatoes, sliced	2–3
1	package alfalfa sprouts	1
1	red onion, very thinly sliced	1
1–2	balls buffalo mozzarella cheese, cut in ½-inch (1 cm) slices	1–2
	Freshly cracked black pepper to taste	
	Chopped fresh herbs (rosemary, basil, oregano, etc.)	
	Crusty Italian bread	

• Place mushrooms in a bowl and cover with hot water. Top with a small plate to keep submerged. Set aside for 10 to 15 minutes.

• In a bowl, whisk together a splash of balsamic vinegar, garlic, Steak Seasoning, and oil.

• Drain the mushrooms caps, pat dry with paper towels, and place on a baking pan, gill side up. Fill each cap with the balsamic mixture and leave to sit for 15 minutes.

• Preheat grill to medium (350ºF/175ºC).

• Carefully set the mushroom caps on the preheated grill and close the lid. Grill-roast for 10 to 15 minutes, or until hot and bubbly. Move caps off the direct heat to a cooler spot if they brown on the bottom too quickly.

• Remove from the grill and keep mushrooms warm.

• Set 2 slices of tomato on a plate and tuck alfalfa sprouts around them. Set a mushroom over and drizzle with olive oil and balsamic vinegar. Top the mushroom with a slice of red onion, then a slice of mozzarella. Top with a mushroom and drizzle again. Sprinkle with cracked pepper and garnish with herbs.

• Serve immediately with crusty Italian bread on the side.

Makes 6 stacks
Prep Time: 30 minutes
Marinade Time: 30 minutes
Cook Time: 15 minutes

FLAMMKUCHEN ON A PLANK
AND BASIC DOUGH FOR PIZZA OR FOCCACIA

2 untreated Napoleon® cedar planks, soaked for 2 to 24 hours; Napoleon® Roasting Pan or 9- by 13-inch (3 L) baking dish, brushed with olive oil

BASIC DOUGH FOR PIZZA OR FOCACCIA

¾ cup	warm water (105º to 115ºF/40º to 46ºC)	175 mL
1 tsp	granulated sugar	5 mL
2½ tsp	active dry yeast	12 mL
1 tbsp	olive oil	15 mL
2 cups	all-purpose flour	500 mL
1 tsp	salt	5 mL
	Oil for the bowl	
1 tbsp	cornmeal	15 mL

TOPPINGS

1	large red onion, peeled, halved, grilled, and sliced thinly	1
6–8	slices bacon, diced and sautéed crisp	6–8
¼ cup	fresh rosemary, very coarsely chopped	60 mL
¾ cup	freshly coarsely shredded Parmesan cheese	175 mL
	Coarse sea salt and freshly cracked pepper to taste	

NOTE: If you like a challenge, try the pizza dough below or buy 1½ pounds (750 g) dough at a bakery or a grocery store and proceed.

TIP: If a planked pizza seems over the top, try the Napoleon® Pizza Pan and perhaps the Smoker Tube and Hickory Chips to ramp up the flavours of your usual pizza.

PIZZA OR FOCACCIA DOUGH: Pour the warm water into a medium bowl. Mix in the sugar until dissolved and then sprinkle the yeast over the surface. Stir to combine and allow to sit for 5 minutes, or until yeast foams. Stir in the olive oil. Add flour and salt and mix well, scraping down the sides of the bowl.

• Turn onto a lightly floured surface and knead until soft and smooth, about 5 minutes. Form the dough into a ball. Grease a large bowl and place the dough into it, rolling to coat with oil. Cover the bowl with a tea towel and place in a warm, draft-free spot to double in bulk, about 1 hour.

FOR PIZZA: Preheat grill to medium-high (450ºF/230ºC). Sprinkle cornmeal on each soaked plank. Punch down the dough to press out air and divide into 2 dough balls. Roll each out to fit prepared soaked planks. Add toppings and bake for about 20 minutes with lid closed, or until crust is browned Pay close attention to crackling sounds and use spray bottle of water if planks begin to burn.

FOR FOCACCIA: Preheat oven or grill to just above medium (400ºF/200ºC). Brush a Napoleon® Roasting Pan or baking dish generously with olive oil. Gently press the risen dough into the prepared pan, smoothing the top then creating small dimples with your fingers. Lightly brush with olive oil and sprinkle with fresh rosemary and coarse salt or topping of your choice. Place the pan on one side of the grill and turn the burner directly under it off. Close the lid and grill/bake until golden brown, about 35 minutes.

Serves 4 to 8
Prep Time: 30 minutes
Dough Rise Time: 1 hour
Cook Time: 35 minutes

SAUSAGE AND PEPPERS ON A BUN

Napoleon® Multi-Grill Basket

1	large red onion, peeled and cut in wedges through the root	1
1	large white onion, peeled and cut in wedges through the root	1
2	green bell peppers, halved, seeded, and cut in ½-inch (1 cm) strips	2
2	red bell peppers, halved, seeded, and cut in ½-inch (1 cm) strips	2
2	yellow bell peppers, halved, seeded, and cut in ½-inch (1 cm) strips	2
1	head garlic, cloves separated and peeled	1
¼ cup	olive oil	60 mL
1 cup	Mango Barbecue Sauce (see recipe, page 50)	250 mL
8–12	assorted fresh sausages, such as hot Italian, mild Italian, bratwurst, chorizo, or andouille	8–12
2 cups	Mango Barbecue Sauce (see recipe, page 50)	500 mL
8–12	crusty Italian buns, sliced in half lengthwise	8–12
½ cup	olive oil	125 mL

Serves 8 to 12
Prep Time: 30 minutes
Cook Time: 30 minutes

• Preheat grill to medium (350°F/175°C).

• Toss onions, peppers and garlic with olive oil to coat and place in a Napoleon® Multi-Grill Basket. Grill for 10 to 15 minutes, turning twice, or until tender and slightly charred. Remove from the grill and toss with the 1 cup (250 mL) Mango Barbecue Sauce.

• While peppers are grilling, place the assorted sausages on the other side of grill. Grill for 6 to 8 minutes, turning occasionally, until thoroughly cooked (an instant-read thermometer should show an internal temperature of 170°F/77°C) and lightly charred.

• While sausages and vegetables are cooking, heat the 2 cups (500 mL) Mango Barbecue sauce in a small saucepan on the side burner.

• Brush cut sides of buns with olive oil. Grill cut sides for 1 to 2 minutes a side, or until lightly browned and crisp.

• Mound the grilled pepper mixture on a bun bottom and arrange the sausage on top. Serve immediately with the warmed Mango Barbecue Sauce.

BEEF

ABOUT STEAKS

• When choosing a steak, or for that matter a roast, look for marbling, colour, moisture, and top grades. Marbling should run evenly through the meat without large clumps. The fat should be milky white, not yellow, brown, or green-tinged. The flesh should have a rich pink or light cherry look. Even a well-aged darker steak will have that red, not brown, tinge hue. If it is very dark or brownish, the meat is likely to be bland and tough. It may have come from a dairy cow, or it may have spent far too long on the shelf. The beef should have a moist surface but not be sticky or outright wet. There should not be much be pooled liquid in a pre packaged cut, as this might indicate previous freezing.

• Buy the best grades you can afford regardless of the cut. Try to buy beef that's been aged for at least 4 to 6 weeks. Dry-aged beef is the best. It's expensive, but the lack of moisture concentrates the flavours. Try to find a good butcher who listens and will work with you. These guys exist even in the large supermarkets, so ask. Even the big club stores can be a surprisingly good source for meat.

• Match the cut to the intention. The premium tenderloin and rib steaks give one result, flank steaks a totally different one.

FLATIRON STEAK, also known as **TOP BLADE STEAK**, is an economical and highly flavourful steak cut from the chuck, or shoulder, section of the forequarter. Chuck is usually associated with stewing and braising cuts, but the flatiron steak is as tender as some of the more premium cuts, while its flavour compares to skirt or hanger steak. Cook it fast over high heat and slice it thin. Make a sauce or a salsa or use one of the myriad of commercially available products.

FLANK STEAK comes from the lower hind region of the animal. It is a tougher cut of meat and does best with marinating. It has little internal fat, so is best cooked fast over high heat to medium rare and sliced across the grain into thin slices for a salad or sandwich.

HANGER STEAK is a muscle that is so called because it hangs independently (as opposed to being connected to a bone — hence the nickname "hanging tender") between the rib and the loin. The flavour is intense and will tolerate strong flavours in a marinade or seasoning. This little-known cut is tender, full of flavour, and very juicy if cooked no more than medium rare and sliced thinly across the grain for serving.

SIRLOIN comes from the area between the short loin and the round. These are very flavourful but well-exercised muscles, so they require a little work to tenderize. Marinades and pounding will benefit this cut.

TENDERLOIN STEAKS are from the large end of a whole tenderloin. The tenderloin lies between the rib and the sirloin and gets no exercise. It is the most tender cut of beef. It has virtually no fat, so it is a tragedy to cook it any more than medium rare to medium.

FILET MIGNON is from the leanest and most tender part of the tenderloin. Usually cut 2 to 3 inches (5 to 7.5 cm) thick, they are best cooked no more than medium rare to give their very best flavour and texture.

T-BONES offer the richness of a strip steak with a portion of the tenderloin all in one cut of steak. Cut from the centre of the short loin, T-bones can be a hearty meal for one or a nice meal for two. The T-bone loves the grill.

PORTERHOUSE STEAK, cut in half through the bone, gives you a bone-in strip steak and a bone-in filet mignon. It is essentially the same cut as the T-bone but with a larger portion of the tenderloin, and it grills beautifully. The best porterhouse is 1½ inches (4 cm) or more thick and weighs 2 lbs (1 kg) or more. A good porterhouse will serve 4 people or more quite nicely.

RIB STEAKS cut from the centre of the rib section between the rib and the chuck are incredibly tender. They have a good amount of rich marbling, which makes them perfect for the high heat of the grill, and the full-bodied flavour and richness that comes from leaving the bone intact. A thick-cut rib steak with the bone frenched is known as a cowboy steak — and grilled medium rare is just this side of paradise.

RIB-EYE is the delicious version of the rib steak with the bone and fat cap removed. Same flavour, same tenderness.

STRIP LOIN comes from the top loin muscle in the short loin of beef. It's one of the most popular cuts of beef, especially in restaurants. The strip loin doesn't have a lot of internal fat so it is best cooked medium-rare to medium. These steaks are definitely grill friendly and are enhanced by butters and light sauces.

BASIC GUIDE TO COOKING A PERFECT STEAK

See instructions for infrared cooking, page 203, for an even more perfect steak.

1. Remove your steaks from the refrigerator at least 30 minutes before cooking. Pat them dry with a paper towel.

2. Preheat grill to high (500°F/260°C).

3. Rub both sides of the steaks with your favourite dry seasoning or coarse kosher or sea salt and freshly ground pepper. Massage the seasoning well into the meat.

4. Place the steaks on the grill and sear the outside to seal in the juices for 2 to 3 minutes a side.

5. Turn grill down to medium-high (450°F/230°C). Brush both sides of steaks with extra-virgin olive oil. This will help form the crust that adds a touch of culinary perfection.

6. Grill a further 3 to 7 minutes a side, to a desired doneness using the timing suggestions in the chart opposite.

7. Transfer the steaks to dinner plates or a platter and let rest 5 minutes before slicing and serving.

Prep Time: 5 minutes
Bring to Room Temp: 30 minutes
Cook Time: 7 to 10 minutes

STEAK TIPS

• A steak for the grill should be about 1 to 1¼ inches (2.5 to 3 cm) thick with no more than ¼ to ½ inch (0.5 to 1 cm) of fat along the side.

• Never pierce a steak or cut into it while cooking. This will allow all the natural juices to flow out, carrying the flavour along with them. A rare steak will feel somewhat soft and yield no juices when pressed; a medium will feel firmer but still have some softness, and juices will just barely break the surface; and a well done will feel firm and yield no juices. Practise using an instant-read meat thermometer to take you to perfection.

• Make sure you have a clean grill. Brush the grill with your wire grill brush before and after you cook anything to avoid transferring off, burnt notes and creating flare-ups.

• Preheat, preheat, preheat. Don't ignore this. Never ever put a steak on a cold grill. And never put an ice-cold steak on a hot grill. Preparation is 99% of perfection.

• After brushing with grill brush, lightly brush or rub the grill with oil before placing the steaks on it.

• Resist the urge to constantly poke and prod the steaks. Set them on the grill and leave them alone until it's time to turn them. Flipping them back and forth slows the cooking and dries the juices up.

• Letting a steak rest before serving is very important. This step should never be ignored; it will allow the juices to spread back out from the centre and give juicy texture to every bite.

• As evidenced by the chart below, cooking times are very subjective. The chart is merely intended to give you a starting point.

STEAK DONENESS CHART (APPROXIMATE MINUTES PER SIDE)

Thickness	RARE 130°F (54°C) to 140°F (60°C)	MEDIUM RARE 140°F (60°C) to 145°F (63°C)	MEDIUM 145°F (63°C) to 150°F (65°C)	MEDIUM WELL 150°F (65°C) to 160°F (71°C)	WELL DONE 160°F (71°C) to 170°F (77°C)
¾ inch (2 cm)	1–2		2–3		3–4
1 inch (2.5 cm)	3–4		4–6		6–7
1½ inches (4 cm)	4–6		6–8		8–9
2 inches (5 cm)	6–8		8–10		9–10

COFFEE-RUBBED GRILLED PORTERHOUSE
WITH A ROASTED GARLIC AND ORANGE VINAIGRETTE

VINAIGRETTE

1 tbsp	Grill-Roasted Garlic (see page 56), mashed	15 mL
1 tsp	kosher salt	5 mL
½ cup	frozen orange juice concentrate, thawed	125 mL
2 tbsp	Dijon mustard	30 mL
¼ cup	freshly squeezed lime juice	60 mL
1 cup	extra-virgin olive oil	250 mL
	Freshly ground black pepper	
2 tbsp	coarsely ground coffee beans	30 mL
2 tbsp	pecans, finely chopped	30 mL
1 tbsp	freshly ground black pepper	15 mL
1 tbsp	unsweetened cocoa powder	15 mL
1½ tsp	kosher salt	7 mL
½ tsp	ground cinnamon	2 mL
2	porterhouse steaks (about 36 oz/1 kg each), 2 inches (5 cm) thick	2
1 tbsp	olive oil	15 mL

VINAIGRETTE: Whisk together the Grill-Roasted Garlic, 1 tsp (5 mL) salt, orange juice concentrate, mustard, and lime juice in a nonreactive bowl. Slowly drizzle in the olive oil, whisking constantly to make an emulsion; season with pepper. Cover and set aside.

• Combine the coffee, pecans, 1 tbsp (15 mL) pepper, cocoa, 1½ tsp (7 mL) salt, and cinnamon and mix well.

• Pat steaks dry with paper towels and rub with the olive oil. Rub the coffee mixture into the steaks all over, massaging and pressing to generously coat with the mixture. Set aside at room temperature for 20 to 30 minutes.

• Preheat the grill to medium-high (450ºF/230ºC).

• Grill the steaks for 8 to 10 minutes a side for medium rare. Remove from the grill and let rest for 3 to 5 minutes.

• Carve the steak in ½-inch (1 cm) slices, and serve over a puddle of the vinaigrette on a platter or individual plates with more sauce on the side.

Serves 4 to 6
Prep Time: 30 minutes
Marinade Time: 30 minutes
Cook Time: 20 to 25 minutes

TIP: Use tongs to lift off the grill. You don't want to pierce or tear the meat while handling and lose all those precious juices.

GRILLED T-BONE STEAK
WITH WHIPPED HORSERADISH CREAM

2	green onions, thinly sliced on the diagonal	2
6 tbsp	extra-hot horseradish, drained but not squeezed dry	90 mL
1 cup	whipping (35%) cream, whipped to stiff peaks	250 mL
	Salt and freshly cracked black pepper	
4	T-bone steaks (about 24 oz/750 g each), 1½ inches (4 cm) thick	
2 tbsp	olive oil	30 mL
¼ cup	Steak Spice (see recipe, page 18)	60 mL
1 tbsp	olive oil	15 mL

• Gently fold the green onions and horseradish into the whipped cream. Season to taste with salt and pepper, cover, and refrigerate until needed.

• Pat steaks dry with paper towels and rub with the olive oil. Rub the Steak Spice into the steaks all over, massaging and pressing to adhere. Set aside at room temperature for 20 to 30 minutes.

• Preheat the grill to medium-high (450ºF/230ºC).

• Grill the steaks for 7 to 9 minutes a side for medium rare. Remove from the grill and let rest for 5 minutes.

• Serve with the horseradish cream on the side.

Serves 4 to 6
Prep Time: 20 minutes
Marinade Time: 30 minutes
Cook Time: 20 minutes

GRILLED RIB-EYE STEAK
WITH ROMESCO SAUCE

6	rib-eye steaks (about 12 oz/375 g each), 1½ inches (4 cm) thick	6
6 tbsp	Garlic and Herb Rub (see recipe, page 26)	90 mL

MARINADE

½ cup	sherry vinegar	125 mL
½ cup	olive oil	125 mL
2 tbsp	freshly cracked black pepper	30 mL

ROMESCO SAUCE

2	4-oz (120 mL) jars fire-roasted pimentos, undrained	2
½ tsp	cayenne pepper	2 mL
1	ripe plum tomato	1
2	slices crusty Italian bread, torn into pieces	2
½ cup	slivered salted almonds	125 mL
2 tbsp	hot Spanish paprika	30 mL
4	cloves garlic, chopped	4
1 tbsp	red wine vinegar	15 mL
2 tsp	sherry vinegar	10 mL
2 tbsp	warm water	30 mL
2 tsp	kosher salt (or to taste)	10 mL
½ cup	extra-virgin olive oil	125 mL
¼ cup	curly parsley, chopped	60 mL

TIP: Romesco Sauce is a traditional Spanish condiment that's superb with grilled meats. Try it with seafood and lamb as well. For a really simple appetizer, serve it with slices of baguette rubbed with grilled garlic.

• Rub steaks with the Garlic and Herb Rub, massaging into the flesh.

• In a glass dish large enough to hold the steaks in a single layer, whisk together the ½ cup (125 mL) sherry vinegar, ½ cup (125 mL) olive oil, and 2 tbsp (30 mL) pepper.

• Add the steaks, turning to coat both sides with the marinade. Cover and refrigerate for 4 hours. Remove from refrigerator 30 to 45 minutes before grilling.

ROMESCO SAUCE: Place the roasted pimentos, cayenne, tomato, bread, almonds, paprika, garlic, red wine vinegar, 2 tsp (10 mL) sherry vinegar, water, and salt into a food processor. Process to a thick purée. With the motor running, slowly pour in the ½ cup (125 mL) olive oil in a steady stream to form a smooth sauce. Cover and let sit at room temperature for at least 1 hour before serving. Will keep in the refrigerator for several weeks.

• Preheat the grill to medium-high (450ºF/230ºC).

• Remove steaks from marinade and brush away excess. Grill for 4 to 5 minutes a side for medium rare. Spoon Romesco Sauce over one end of the steak and garnish with parsley. Serve with more sauce on the side.

Serves 6
Prep Time: 45 minutes
Marinade Time: 4 hours
Cook Time: 10 minutes

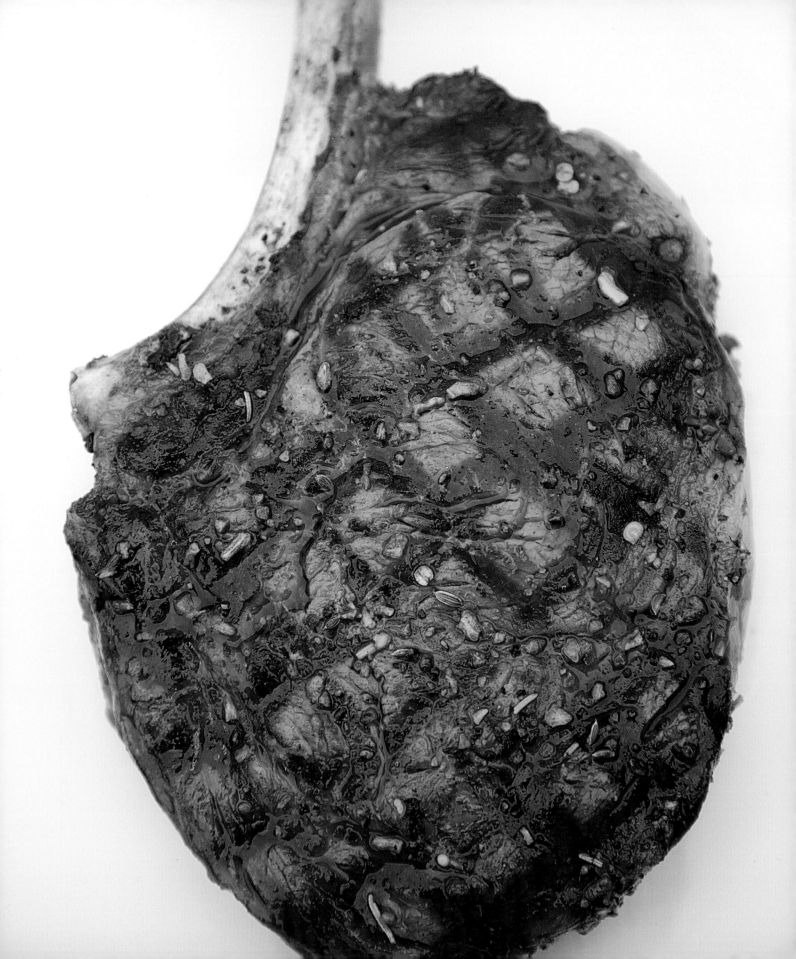

COWBOY STEAK
WITH MUSHROOMS, ONIONS, AND GORGONZOLA

2	bone-in cowboy (rib) steaks (24 oz/750 g each), 2 to 3 inches (5 to 7.5 cm) thick	2
¼ cup	Steak Spice (see recipe, page 18)	60 mL
¼ cup	Grill-Roasted Garlic (see recipe, page 56), divided	60 mL
2 tbsp	unsalted butter	30 mL
1	medium onion, halved, then thinly sliced	1
3 cups	mushrooms (field, brown, and/or shiitake)	750 mL
2 tbsp	balsamic vinegar	30 mL
1 tbsp	chopped fresh basil	15 mL
	Salt and freshly ground black pepper	
1 cup	Gorgonzola cheese	250 mL
	Fresh basil leaves (optional)	

• Rub the steaks with the Steak Spice and about 2 tbsp/ 30 mL of the Grill-Roasted Garlic. Massage well, mashing the roasted garlic to spread all over the meat surfaces. Place on a plate, cover, and let sit at room temperature for at least 30 minutes to marinate. If not using right away, refrigerate.

• Preheat the grill to medium-high (450ºF/230ºC).

• In a pan or wok on the side burner, melt the butter over medium-high heat. Sauté the onions for 2 to 3 minutes, or until tender and beginning to turn translucent. Add all the mushrooms and sauté for 8 to 10 minutes, stirring occasionally, until tender, and the moisture has evaporated. Stir in the vinegar, chopped basil, and the rest of the Grill-Roasted Garlic and cook, stirring, until vinegar has been absorbed. Season to taste with salt and pepper and set aside to keep warm.

• Grill steaks for 8 to 12 minutes a side for medium-rare (or for 4 to 6 minutes on the infrared grid). Let rest 5 minutes.

• Slice the steaks and set on a platter. Top with the onion mixture, crumble the Gorgonzola over all, garnish with basil leaves, if desired, and serve immediately.

Serves 4 to 6
Prep Time: 30 minutes
Marinade Time: 30 minutes
Cook Time: 40 minutes

GRILLED SIRLOIN STEAK
WITH CARAMELIZED ONIONS AND MUSHROOMS

Napoleon® Round or Square Wok Topper

6	cloves garlic, puréed	6
1 tbsp	Dijon mustard	15 mL
1	sirloin steak (about 3 lb/1.5 kg), trimmed	1
	Salt and freshly ground black pepper	
3 tbsp	butter	45 mL
2 tbsp	olive oil	30 mL
2	large sweet onions, peeled and trimmed, thinly sliced	2
1 lb	large white mushrooms, quartered	500 g
4	cloves garlic, minced	3
¼ cup	red wine vinegar	60 mL
1 tbsp	granulated sugar	15 mL
	Salt and freshly ground black pepper	

• Combine the garlic purée and mustard. Place the steak on a flat surface and pat dry with paper towels, then massage the garlic mixture into the steak. Season the steak with salt and pepper. Cover and set aside at room temperature for 30 to 45 minutes.

• Preheat the grill to medium-high (450ºF/230ºC).

• Place the wok — or a heavy sauté pan — on the side burner and heat over a high flame. Melt the butter and olive oil to sizzling and add the sliced onions. Sauté to soften, about 3 to 4 minutes. Add the mushrooms and continue sautéing until the mushrooms have softened and any moisture has evaporated. Stir in the minced garlic, sauté for another 3 minutes, and then move pan over to the grill. Let the mixture slow-sauté over the grill, stirring frequently, until the onions have turned a deep golden brown, about 15 minutes. Do not let the onions brown too fast or they will burn instead of caramelizing.

• Add the vinegar and stir until it is absorbed. Stir in the sugar and season with salt and pepper. Set the onion mixture aside and keep warm.

• Place the steak on the grill and cook for 5 to 6 minutes a side for medium rare. Remove from the grill and let rest for 3 to 4 minutes.

• Thinly slice the steak across the grain. Place slices on a platter or individual plates and top with the onion mixture. Serve immediately.

Serves 4 to 6
Prep Time: 30 minutes
Marinade Time: 30 to 45 minutes
Cook Time: 45 minutes

GRILLED FLANK STEAK
WITH THAI MARINADE AND PEANUT SAUCE

THAI MARINADE

½ cup	soy sauce	125 mL
½ cup	freshly squeezed lime juice	125 mL
2 tbsp	crunchy peanut butter	30 mL
1 tbsp	palm sugar or brown sugar	15 mL
1 tbsp	Madras curry powder	15 mL
3	cloves garlic, minced	3
1	red chile, seeded and minced	1
2 lbs	flank steak	1 kg
	Peanut Sauce	
	(see recipe, page 92)	

THAI MARINADE: In a nonreactive bowl, whisk together the soy sauce, lime juice, peanut butter, palm sugar, curry powder, garlic, and chile.

• Place the steak in a nonreactive dish large enough to hold the meat in one layer. Pour the marinade over and turn to coat the steak well. Cover and refrigerate for a minimum of 4 hours or overnight.

• Prepare the Peanut Sauce.

• Pour the marinade off the steak and into a saucepan. Set the steak aside to come to room temperature. Bring the marinade to a full rolling boil for 2 to 3 minutes, then remove from the heat and set aside to use as a baste.

• Preheat the grill to medium-high (450°F/230°C).

• Grill the flank steak for about 8 to 10 minutes a side for medium rare, basting with the marinade. Remove from the grill to a clean cutting board and let rest for 5 to 7 minutes. Slice across the grain into thin slices.

• Serve the steak slices with Barbecue-Fried Rice (see recipe, page 81) or noodles and lots of Peanut Sauce.

Serves 6 to 8
Prep Time: 30 minutes
Marinade Time: 4 hours to overnight
Cook Time: 30 minutes

TIP: Memorize this: Bring ingredients to room temperature. The grill is hot. Even a grill on low is hot by any other standard. Food, expecially meat, with a cold centre will never cook evenly.

ABOUT ROASTS

Some of the most popular cuts for the grill are listed below. The best results come from the cuts on the loin, short loin, and rib, but the tougher front and back cuts can be enhanced by the grill as well.

PRIME RIB is cut off the front of the loin. This cut can have four to seven ribs and weigh up to 22 lbs (10 kg). The best come from the short end, the 12th through 17th ribs. Richly marbled, this roast makes for a magnificent presentation off the grill. A four-rib roast will serve 4 to 6 and each additional rib will add 2 servings. Mastering the technique is surprisingly easy, whether using direct or indirect heat. If using direct heat methods, the meat will need constant attention to avoid fat flare-ups and burning, but it is almost impossible to ruin a prime rib using indirect or rotisserie methods.

RIB-EYE is a boneless prime rib, with lots of rich marbling. A full-size rib-eye will run between 10 and 14 lbs (4.5 to 6 kg). The fat content means that, like a prime rib, this cut will roast beautifully on the grill or rotisserie. A little wood smoke will enhance the flavour and impress the crowd. As with the prime rib, these roasts need a good deal of attention for a good result, but are indeed worth the effort.

STRIP LOIN is off the top loin. A whole strip loin will roast or smoke beautifully with care. As with the steaks, the internal fat content is limited, so they're best seared and served rare to medium rare. The results can be excellent.

TENDERLOIN is the emperor of beef. It is very pricey, but when you consider this most tender of cuts, remember that you will not lose more than a very few ounces to trim. Every part is edible, compared with a prime rib, where you will lose as much as 50% of the roast to ribs and fat. At most you will have to slip a very sharp knife blade under the thin silver skin and gently shave it away from the surface although most tenderloins are fully trimmed before purchase these days. A whole tenderloin has a rich but delicate flavour and will roast relatively quickly, so it is very important not to overcook.

TOP SIRLOIN, bottom sirloin (tri-tip), and sirloin tip are flavour filled though slightly less tender than cuts from the loin. Treated properly, they can be quite tender. They are at their best rare to medium rare and like marinades and stronger flavourings. They can be done on the rotisserie to great result, especially with a rich oily baste.

EYE OF ROUND and **INSIDE ROUND** are hind end cuts that tend to be flavourful but tough. They require marinating if roasted whole and do best with slow, moist cooking or smoking. These cuts are often roasted and sliced thinly across the grain for fajitas and sandwiches or salads. Ground beef for burgers also come from this end of the animal.

BRISKET, slow-roasted with lots of smoke, is a thing to behold. Cut from the bottom front of the animal, this is a very tough cut. Cooked rare or even to medium, it is quite simply inedible. But very long, slow roasting with moisture and smoke will yield an addictive result.

ROASTING TIPS

• Patience. Roast on your grill with or without smoke, with direct or indirect heat, on the rotisserie or in a roasting pan, using a marinade or rub or both. Choose the recipe well and follow it to the letter. The recipes in this book are designed to give you the principles that will allow you to understand the meat and begin to create your own style.

• Invest in a couple of good-quality sharp knives and a steel to hone their edges. Dull knives play havoc with expensive cuts of meat and are far more likely to cause accidents. You need a good carving knife and fork if you're going to be able to serve the perfect roast you just spent all afternoon preparing.

• Preheat, preheat, preheat. Don't ignore this. Never put a roast into a cold barbecue.

• A roast should be brought to room temperature before going on the grill. This is even more important for a roast than for a steak. A cold roast will lower the temperature in the grill, and instead of a sear, you will just leach out juices as the grill recovers. It's also important that the temperature at the centre of a roast be even with the outside so you don't end up with an overdone outside and a blue-rare centre. You can use your instant-read thermometer to check for a minimum of 65°F (18°C) at the centre. Remember that the roast will continue to cook as it rests.

• Use a drip pan when roasting on the grill. This prevents flare-ups and provides the basic ingredient for a great sauce. With tougher cuts, add some water, wine, beer, etc., to the pan to provide additional moisture to the roast.

• As mentioned with steaks, get an instant-read thermometer. It is an absolute must with roasts. Your Napoleon® dealer has an excellent selection, and an instant-read thermometer should be included in your initial purchase. It is as necessary as the propane tank.

• Letting the roast rest after removing it from the heat is absolutely essential for the best results and allows the juices to even out. Don't ignore this step — factor it into the timing for serving your meal. Just cover with foil and relax. Not only will the roast not cool down, it will continue to cook for at least another 15 minutes on the reserved internal heat without losing any of the precious juices.

• Invest in a Napoleon® Roasting Pan and Roasting Rack to extend your possibilities. Large cuts of beef can do very well seared over the high heat of the infrared grill and then moved into the pan to roast under a closed lid.

THE BASICS FOR GRILLING
A PERFECT PRIME RIB ROAST

1 lb (500 g) Napoleon® Smoker Wood Chips (hickory, cherry, etc.), soaked for 30 minutes

Butcher's twine for tying roast

Disposable aluminum pan

Napoleon® Roasting Rack and Roasting Pan

1	prime rib roast, 3 to 7 ribs from the short end, bones removed from the meat in one piece, outside fat trimmed to ¼ to ⅛ inch (0.5 to 0.25 cm)	1
1 tbsp	vegetable oil	15 mL
	Freshly ground black pepper	
¼ cup	kosher salt	60 mL
½ cup	extra-virgin olive oil	125 mL
¼ cup	minced fresh garlic,	60 mL
¼ cup	chopped rosemary	60 mL

See infrared instructions, page 203, for grilling the perfect rotisserie prime rib.

Everyone with a grill feels quite unperturbed about grilling steaks, chops, burgers, and hot dogs. Cooking a roast on the grill can seem like a daunting task, but it's easier than you think. As mentioned over and over in this book, preparation is key. The biggest difference between grilling a steak or a roast is the time required to bring it to perfection, The juiciest and most tender roast you can imagine, with unique flavours only cooking with smoke and flame can impart, awaits you. And once this skill is mastered, you will never do it any other way.

• Rub roast with vegetable oil and season generously with pepper. Rub all over evenly with the salt, pressing into the meat so it adheres. Lay meat back on the bones exactly as it was and tie tightly in place between each set of bones with two lengths of twine, using strong knots.

• Refrigerate, uncovered, for 1 hour and then let sit at room temperature for 2 hours.

• Drain wood chips and place in the aluminium pan.

• Preheat grill on all burners to high (500ºF/260ºC) with the lid down.

• Sear roast on fat-covered sides until well browned. Do not brown the meaty ends. This should take 8 to 10 minutes unless you have an infrared burner. (If you do, heat it to very high before searing. You should get a very nicely browned roast in about 5 minutes.)

• Turn off all but one side of the grill. Place the aluminium pan of wood chips over this burner.

• Combine the olive oil, garlic, and rosemary and mix to a paste. Rub well all over the seared roast.

• Place the seared roast, bone side down, on the Napoleon® Roasting Rack and set the roasting pan on the cool side of the grill. Close the lid.

• Grill-roast for at least 2 to 2½ hours (15 to 20 minutes a pound). Resist the urge

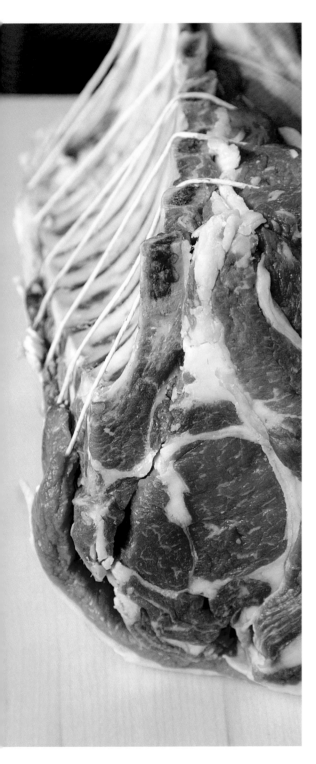

to lift the lid and lose the heat inside for at least 1½ hours, and 2 hours is better. Remove the roast from the barbecue when a meat thermometer inserted into the centre reads 135ºF (57ºC) for medium-rare.

• Seal the roast in foil loosely and let rest for 20 to 30 minutes. Residual heat will continue the cooking process as the roast rests and evens out its juices.

• Cut away the twine, remove the roast from the bones, and carve. Serve immediately. If you are preparing a sauce or jus, save the abundance of juices to add to it.

Prep Time: 10 minutes
Bring Room Temp: 1 hour
Cook Time: 2 to 3 hours

PRIME RIB NOTES

• The butcher in most good stores will be happy to separate the bones from the roast for you.

• The initial rub of kosher salt helps develop a crunchy crust from the combination of a good sear and roasting over indirect heat. Allowing the roast to sit with the salt coating it for 2 to 3 hours will draw just enough moisture from under the surface of the meat to promote a good sear. But let it sit for too long and you will draw too much moisture from the roast and defeat your purpose.

• The garlic, oil, and rosemary paste gives a wonderful traditional crust to the roast. Feel free to play with this formula. Add puréed chipotle peppers and a bit of the adobo sauce they are preserved in, or mix in your own favourite herbs and/or seasoning mixes. Keep in mind that the seasoning on a prime rib is going to penetrate only about ¼ to ½ inches (0.5 to 1 cm) and should not compete too much with the smoke notes and the delicate flavour of the meat.

• Expect to lose 50 percent of a Prime Rib to bones, fat, and cooking loss. Six to 8 ounces of cooked meat per person is average so a 6 lb (2.7 kg) roast will serve 6 to 8.

THE ROTISSERIE PRIME RIB ROAST

Butcher's twine for tying roast
Disposable aluminum pan
Napoleon® Rotisserie

1	prime rib roast, 3 to 7 ribs from the short end, bones removed from the meat in one piece, outside fat trimmed to ¼ to ⅛ inch (0.5 to 0.25 cm)	1
	Freshly ground black pepper and kosher salt	
½ cup	extra-virgin olive oil	125 mL
¼ cup	fresh garlic, minced	60 mL
¼ cup	rosemary, chopped	60 mL
2–4 cups	beer, wine, or water	500 mL –1 L

• Season the roast generously with black pepper and kosher salt or your favourite seasoning, pressing into the meat so it adheres. Lay meat back on the bones exactly as it was and tie tightly in place between each set of bones with two lengths of twine, using strong knots.

• Let sit at room temperature for 2 hours.

• Follow the manufacturer's instructions to secure the meat on the rotisserie rod, taking care to make sure the forks are secure and the meat's weight is evenly distributed so it will turn evenly. An unbalanced roast can burn out your motor.

• Preheat the rotisserie burner to high.

• Fix the rotisserie rod onto the grill and check to be sure it's secure. Turn on the motor and watch for a few moments to be certain it's rotating smoothly. If not, take it off and readjust to balance the roast.

• Let the meat sear for 15 to 20 minutes with the lid open. Turn the heat down to medium and close the lid. The temperature gauge on the hood should read between 275ºF (135ºC) and 300ºF (150ºC).

- Combine the olive oil, garlic, and rosemary and mix to a paste. Brush all over the seared roast. Place the aluminum pan below the roast and add 2 cups (500 mL) of the beer (add more if it evaporates).

- Rotisserie-roast for at least 2 to 2½ hours (15 to 20 minutes a pound). Resist the urge to lift the lid and lose the heat inside for at least 1½ hours; 2 hours is better.

- Check for doneness by turning motor off periodically and carefully inserting a meat thermometer in the centre without making contact with the rotisserie rod. Remember that when you open the lid, you lose a lot of heat that must be recovered once you close it again. Be patient. If the meat isn't done, close the lid for at least 20 to 30 minutes before you check again.

- Remove the roast from the barbecue when a meat thermometer inserted into the centre reads 135ºF (57ºC) for medium-rare.

- When the roast is done, remove it carefully from the grill, using gloves. Then remove the forks and rod.

- Seal the roast in foil loosely and let rest for 20 to 30 minutes. Residual heat will continue the cooking process as the roast rests and evens out its juices.

- Cut away the twine, remove the roast from the bones, and carve. Serve immediately.

- The drip pan below the roast should be full of a delicious liquid. With the juices that run from the roast as it is carved, you will have a great jus or the start of a fabulous gravy or sauce (see recipe below).

- Enjoy!

PRIME RIB PAN DRIPPINGS GRAVY

½ cup	beef fat from drippings	125 mL
¼ cup	all-purpose flour	60 mL
	drippings from roast, skimmed of fat	
1 cup	red wine	250 mL
	Salt and freshly ground black pepper	

- Pour beef fat into a large saucepan. Heat over medium-high heat to a sizzle and stir in the flour to make a paste.

- Pour in the wine and the drippings from the roast and bring to a boil, whisking until smooth. Let simmer for 5 minutes to cook out the flour. If the gravy is too thick or there weren't enough drippings, add liquid (water, wine, beef stock, or a combination).

- Season with salt and pepper. The flavour of the best gravies comes from the meat. Try not to overseason it and defeat the natural flavours.

Serves 6 to 8
Prep Time: 10 minutes
Cook Time: at least 10 minutes on the simmer

GRILLED WHOLE BEEF TENDERLOIN
WITH COGNAC BUTTER

Napoleon® Cajun Injector

½ cup	unsalted butter, melted and cooled	125 mL
¼ cup	cognac	60 mL
1 tbsp	fresh thyme, chopped finely	15 mL
1	beef tenderloin, about 3 lb (1.5 kg), silver skin trimmed (see Roasting Tips Page 183)	1
¼ cup	Steak Spice (see recipe, page 18)	60 mL
1 tbsp	smoked paprika (available in specialty stores)	15 mL
2 tbsp	olive oil	30 mL

COGNAC BUTTER SAUCE

1 tbsp	butter	15 mL
6	shallots, peeled and sliced thinly	6
4	cloves garlic, minced	4
2 tbsp	cognac	30 mL
6 tbsp	cold butter, broken into 1-tsp (5 ml) size chunks	90 mL
	Salt and freshly ground black pepper	

• Whisk together the melted butter, cognac, and thyme until well combined.

• Place tenderloin on a flat surface and pat dry with paper towels. Fill the injector with the Cognac Butter mixture. Stab and inject the tenderloin in multiple places. Cover in plastic wrap and refrigerate for 2 hours.

• Mix the Steak Spice and smoked paprika. Remove tenderloin from the refrigerator and rub with the olive oil, and then massage well with the spice mixture. Set aside for 30 minutes to come to room temperature.

• Cognac Butter Sauce: Meanwhile, place a small saucepan on the side burner of the grill and heat the 1 tbsp (15 mL) of butter just to a sizzle. Add the shallots and garlic and sauté for 3 to 4 minutes, until very soft and fragrant. Stir in the 2 tbsp (30 mL) cognac and carefully allow to flame. Once the flame subsides, remove from the heat and whisk the cold butter into the mixture, one chunk at a time. If the mixture cools too much to melt the butter, place it back on the burner for a few seconds, but never stop the whisking or the butter sauce will split. Season with salt and pepper and set in a warm spot, but not over direct heat, to wait for the beef.

• Preheat the grill to medium-high (450ºF/230ºC). Preheat the infrared burner for 1 minute.

• Place the beef tenderloin on the infrared burner and sear quickly, about 1½ minutes a side.

• Move tenderloin over to the medium-high side and grill for about 4 to 7 minutes a side for medium rare. Remove from grill and let rest for 5 minutes.

• Place the tenderloin on a carving platter and drizzle the Cognac Butter Sauce over. Serve.

Serves 6 to 8
Prep Time: 30 minutes
Marinade Time: 2½ hours
Cook Time: 20 minutes

GRILL-ROASTED EYE OF ROUND, KOREAN STYLE

MARINADE

¾ cup	Korean soy sauce (available at Asian markets)	175 mL
¼ cup	dry sherry	60 mL
2 tbsp	dark Asian sesame oil	30 mL
6–8	cloves garlic, minced	6–8
1	1-inch (2.5 cm) piece fresh ginger, peeled and minced	1
	Foodsafe plastic bag, large enough to hold roast	
1	eye of round roast (4 lbs/1.8 kg)	1
	Disposable aluminium pan	

SAUCE

¾ cup	Korean soy sauce	175 mL
¾ cup	packed brown sugar	175 mL
2 tbsp	fresh garlic, minced	30 mL
1	1-inch (2.5 cm) piece fresh ginger, peeled and minced	1
¼ cup	green onions, minced	60 mL
1 tbsp	toasted sesame oil	15 mL
	Toasted sesame seeds	

The traditional way to serve this dish is with Bibb lettuce leaves. The sliced beef is placed on a leaf and topped with sesame seeds and perhaps minced hot peppers or kimchi (Korean hot pickle), then the whole thing is rolled and consumed.

MARINADE: In a bowl, combine all the marinade ingredients and mix well.

• Pat the roast dry with paper towels and place in the plastic bag. Pour the marinade into the bag, squeeze out all the air, and seal. Massage the bag to smear the marinade all over the roast and to begin working it into the meat. Refrigerate for at least 8 hours or overnight.

SAUCE: In a saucepan, combine the soy, brown sugar, garlic, and ginger and heat, stirring, just until the sugar is fully dissolved. Remove from the heat and stir in the green onions and sesame oil. Set aside to serve warm or at room temperature.

• Preheat one side of the grill to high (500ºF/260ºC).

• Remove roast from the plastic bag and brush the marinade off. Discard marinade.

• Sear the roast all over, about 2 minutes a side. Turn the grill down to medium-high (450ºF/230ºC) and place the aluminium pan under the cool side of the grill. Move the roast over the pan and close the lid.

• Roast with the lid down for 1½ hours for medium-rare. Eye of round is best grilled no further than medium (155ºF/70ºC).

• Remove from the grill and wrap loosely in foil to rest for 20 to 30 minutes before carving.

• Whisk drippings into the sauce.

• Carve in thin slices and serve immediately with the sauce on the side.

Serves 6 to 8
Prep Time: 30 minutes
Marinade Time: 8 hours to overnight
Cook Time: 1½ to 2 hours

PLANK-SMOKED BEEF TENDERLOIN
WITH SMOKY MASHED POTATOES

2 or 3 untreated Napoleon® 12-inch cedar planks, soaked overnight

SMOKY MASHED POTATOES

8	large Yukon Gold potatoes, peeled and quartered	8
½ cup	table (18%) cream	125 mL
2 tbsp	butter, softened	30 mL
	Salt and freshly ground black pepper to taste	
¼ cup	chopped fresh parsley and/or fresh chives	60 mL
6	beef tenderloin steaks (8 oz/250 g each)	6
¼ cup	Steak Spice (see recipe, page 18)	60 mL
3	8-oz (250 g) wheels brie, sliced in half horizontally	3
	Cajun Creole Seasoning and Rub (see recipe, page 17)	

SMOKY MASHED POTATOES: The day before serving, cook potatoes until quite tender in a large pot of salted boiling water, about 20 to 25 minutes. Drain well and set in a warm spot for 10 to 15 minutes to dry out.

• Meanwhile, combine the cream and butter in the pot and warm slightly. Return the potatoes and mash together with the cream mixture, seasoning with salt and pepper and the chopped herbs. Take care not to overmash — there should be some lumps.

• Set aside to cool to room temperature, cover, and refrigerate overnight.

• When ready to finish, preheat grill to high (500°F/260°F).

• Season steaks with Steak Spice, massaging well into the meat.

• Sear steaks for 2 to 3 minutes a side.

• Lower grill temperature to medium-high (450°F/230°C). Place the seared steaks on one of the presoaked cedar planks. Set on the preheated grill and plank-roast for 20 minutes over indirect heat with the lid closed.

• Form the chilled potatoes into uniform, level mounds on the other soaked plank(s), set on the grill, and plank-roast for 20 minutes over indirect heat with the lid closed.

• Remove the planked steaks and potatoes from the grill. Increase the grill temperature to high (500°F/260°F).

• Place each steak on top of a mound of potatoes and then top each steak with a half-wheel of the Brie. Sprinkle with Cajun Creole Seasoning and Rub return to the grill. Roast over direct heat for 5 to 7 minutes, or until the cheese is melted and the potatoes are golden brown and have formed a crisp crust.

• Carefully remove the smoking planks from the barbecue and move the steak and potatoes to an unused plank, a heatproof platter, or directly to plates to serve immediately.

Serves 6
Prep Time: 45 minutes
Cook Time: 25 minutes

SMOKED BEEF BRISKET

2–3 bags Napoleon® Smoker Hickory Wood Chips,
          soaked for 6 to 8 hours
Napoleon® Smoker Tube
Napoleon® Roasting Pan

1	beef brisket (about 8 to 10 lbs/4 to 5 kg), trimmed, deckle off, outside fat trimmed to about ¼ inch (0.5 cm) thick	1
8 cups	Beer Marinade (see recipe, page 30)	2 L
⅓ cup	Steak Spice (see recipe, page 18)	75 mL
2–4 cups	your favourite barbecue sauce	500 mL –1 L

Beef brisket requires extreme patience and determination. If you have these qualities in abundance, try this. It's well worth the effort, and may make you a legend. Read this recipe very carefully before you attempt a brisket.

• Rinse brisket in cold water and place in a deep container. Pour the Beer Marinade over to fully submerge. Cover tightly and refrigerate for 48 hours.

• The day of cooking, pack the smoker tube with the presoaked wood chips.

• Remove brisket from marinade and discard marinade. Rub meat well with the Steak Spice. Place in the roasting pan, fat side up, cover loosely with plastic wrap, and let sit for 1 hour or more to come to room temperature.

• Preheat grill to high (500ºF/260ºC).

• Turn off the right side. Set the smoker tube on the left-hand burner. Set the roaster pan with the brisket, uncovered, on the right-hand, "cool" burner. Close the lid.

• Adjust the heat to maintain the grill at no more than 225ºF (110°C). Smoke-grill the brisket for 7 to 8 hours. Every hour or so, replace the wood chips in the smoker tube with fresh presoaked chips, trying not to leave the lid open for longer than absolutely necessary to minimize fluctuations in the heat.

• After 7 to 8 hours, take the brisket out of the grill and wrap the roasting pan with a double layer of heavy-duty foil to seal it tight. Return the pan to the grill and continue cooking at the low temperature for another 4 to 6 hours.

• Remove the pan from the grill and let sit for 30 minutes before unwrapping. It should be very, very tender — best carved with an electric knife or shredded.

• Serve with lots of barbecue sauce and good bread, and perhaps Barbecue Baked Beans (see recipe, page 74) and Creamy Coleslaw (see recipe, page 118).

TIP: The deckle on a brisket is a thin layer of meat, fat, and connective tissue on the underside of the brisket. It is easily removed and adds no real value to the brisket. Your butcher will do this for you but make sure he doesn't trim all the fat from the rest of the meat. You want fat to melt into the meat during the long slow cook.

Serves 8 to 12
Prep Time: 30 minutes
Marinade Time: 48 hours
Cook Time: 12 to 14 hours

BRISKET TIPS

• Make sure you begin with a full tank of gas. The cooking time is long, and you don't want to have to be shutting down the grill to change tanks in the middle of the process. *But* do shut down the grill completely if you should have to change the tank!

• Don't try a whole brisket (18 to 22 lbs/8 to 10 kg) in your gas grill. The cooking time would be measured in half-days rather than hours. Also don't try this with a small 2- or 3-lb (1 to 1.5 kg) piece of brisket with all the fat trimmed either. A 10- to 12-lb (4 to 5 kg) brisket with the deckle removed and some of the fat trimmed is perfect for our task. You need some fat to keep the meat moist as it slowly melts in the low temperatures, but not so thick a layer that the smoke can't penetrate to the meat and give you the coveted smoke ring all pit masters want on their brisket.

• Brisket can be frozen for up to 6 weeks. Be sure to wrap it airtight.

GRILLED HAWAIIAN BEEF SHORT RIBS
WITH MOLASSES AND ONION MARMALADE

Heavy foodsafe plastic bag large enough to hold ribs

MARINADE

2 cups	dry red wine	500 mL
½ cup	fancy molasses	125 mL
¼ cup	Worcestershire sauce	60 mL
¼ cup	Dijon mustard	60 mL
¼ cup	Garlic and Herb Rub (see recipe, page 26)	60 mL
4–5 lbs	beef short ribs, cut across the bone, 1 inch (2.5 cm) thick	2–2.2 kg

ONION MARMALADE

2 tbsp	extra-virgin olive oil	30 mL
2 tbsp	salted butter	30 mL
3–4	large red onions, peeled, root removed and cut lengthwise into ¼-inch (0.5 cm) slices	3–4
2 tbsp	apple juice concentrate, thawed	30 mL
¼ cup	cider vinegar	60 mL
1 cup	ginger marmalade	250 mL
	Salt and freshly ground black pepper to taste	
2 cups	Grill-Roasted Garlic Barbecue Sauce (see recipe, page 47)	500 mL

Serves 4 to 6
Prep Time: 30 minutes
Marinade Time: 24 hours
Cook Time: 2 hours

Cut from the chuck, nicely marbled, and meaty, these short ribs are also called Hawaiian ribs. We're not sure why, but we do know they're delicious slow-cooked on the grill. Ask your butcher to cut yours 1 inch (2.5 cm) thick for the extra meatiness.

MARINADE: In a bowl, whisk together the red wine, molasses, Worcestershire sauce, mustard, and Garlic and Herb Rub.

• Trim the ribs of any excess fat. Rinse in cold water and pat dry with paper towels. Place the ribs in the bag. Pour the marinade over them and seal the bag, squeezing out any excess air. Massage to coat the ribs. Place the bag in a bowl and refrigerate for 24 hours.

ONION MARMALADE: In a large heavy skillet, heat the olive oil and butter over medium-low heat. Add the onions and cook slowly, stirring frequently. Reduce heat slightly if onions begin to brown too quickly. Slow-cook the onions for about 30 to 45 minutes, until they have slowly gone from golden to dark caramelized brown without burning. They should have a toasty, sweet, and caramelized flavour.

• Stir in the apple juice concentrate, the vinegar, and ginger marmalade. Allow to simmer until most of the moisture has evaporated and the consistency is that of a marmalade. Season with salt and pepper and pour into a container. Press a piece of wax paper onto the surface of the marmalade to prevent a skin from forming.

• Preheat grill to high (500°F/260°C).

• Remove ribs from the bag. Reserve about 1 cup (250 mL) of the marinade and discard the rest.

• Turn off the right-hand burner and place the ribs on it. Close the lid.

• Adjust the heat on the left-hand burner to maintain 325°F (160°C). Grill the ribs for 1½ to 2 hours, or until very tender, basting occasionally with the reserved marinade until the ribs are about 30 minutes from done.

• Brush the ribs lightly with the Fire-Roasted Barbecue Sauce 2 or 3 times during the last 30 minutes to glaze them.

• Place the ribs on a platter and serve with the onion marmalade and more sauce.

GRAPE-VINE-SKEWERED BEEF KEBABS
WITH A TUSCAN-STYLE SALSA CRUDA

Baking sheet

1¼ cups	Garlic and Herb Rub (see recipe, page 26)	300 mL
1 cup	assorted chopped herbs (rosemary, thyme, parsley, sage, etc.)	250 mL
1	beef tenderloin (about 5 lbs/2.2 kg), trimmed of any excess fat and silver skin	1
16–18	grape vine twigs, about 12 to 16 inches (30 to 40 cm) long, or long heavy rosemary stems	16–18

TUSCAN-STYLE SALSA CRUDA

6–8	large ripe Roma tomatoes, finely diced	6–8
2 tbsp	good-quality fruity extra-virgin olive oil	30 mL
2 tbsp	capers, drained and coarsely chopped if large	30 mL
	Coarse sea salt to taste	
2 tbsp	good-quality balsamic vinegar	30 mL
¼ cup	fresh basil, coarsely chopped	60 mL

• Place the Garlic and Herb Rub on the baking sheet. Pour the chopped herbs on top and thoroughly mix the rub and herbs; spread out over the baking sheet.

• Cut the tenderloin into large cubes, about 1½ to 2 inches (4 to 5 cm), and place the cubes on top of the herbs on the baking sheet. Using your hands, massage the cubes with the rub and herb mixture, pressing into the meat until all the cubes are generously coated.

• Skewer the beef cubes on the vine twigs, about 6 to 8 cubes to a skewer, packed firmly against each other but not squeezed so tightly as to squash the cubes. Pat the rub coating back onto the cubes anywhere it falls away as you skewer.

• Line the skewers up on the baking sheet, cover with plastic wrap, and refrigerate for 2 to 3 hours. Remove the tray from the refrigerator 1 hour before grilling and let sit to come to room temperature.

TUSCAN-STYLE SALSA CRUDA: While skewers are marinating, combine the tomatoes, olive oil, capers, sea salt, balsamic vinegar, and basil and toss well. Cover and set aside to let flavours blend.

• Preheat the grill to medium-high (450ºF/230ºC).

• Grill the skewers on the preheated grill for 3 to 4 minutes a side for medium-rare. Do not overcook beef tenderloin. Serve with the salsa and Grilled Cheese Baguette with Roasted Garlic and Herb Butter (see recipe, page 78).

Serves 6 to 8
Prep Time: 45 minutes
Marinade Time: 4 hours
Cook Time: 10 minutes

SMOKED BEEF RIBS
WITH HONEY, ORANGE, AND CHIPOTLE SAUCE

1 bag Napoleon® Smoker Wood Chips, soaked
        Napoleon® Smoker Tube

8	cloves garlic, minced	8
1½ tbsp	kosher salt	22 mL
1 tbsp	freshly cracked black pepper	15 mL
2 tbsp	chipotle powder	30 mL
2	racks beef ribs (about 3½ lb/1.75 kg)	2
3 cups	beer	750 mL
4 cups	orange juice	1 L

HONEY, ORANGE, AND CHIPOTLE SAUCE

2 tbsp	vegetable oil	30 mL
1	small onion, finely diced	1
5	cloves garlic, minced	5
2	poblano chiles, chopped	2
4	chipotle chiles in adobo sauce (available in most grocery stores)	4
6 tbsp	tomato paste	90 mL
⅔ cup	liquid honey	150 mL
⅔ cup	orange juice	150 mL
½ cup	packed brown sugar	125 mL
¼ cup	cider vinegar	60 mL
1 tbsp	Worcestershire sauce	15 mL
1 tsp	mesquite liquid smoke	5 mL

Serves 4 to 6
Prep Time: 30 minutes
Marinade Time: 24 hours
Cook Time: 3 hours

• In a bowl, combine the garlic, salt, black pepper, and chipotle powder.

• Split the ribs into pieces with 2 or 3 bones each and rub the garlic mixture on all sides. Place the ribs in a large roasting pan and pour the beer and the 4 cups (1 L) orange juice over them. Cover the pan and refrigerate for 24 hours.

HONEY, ORANGE, AND CHIPOTLE SAUCE: Heat the oil over medium heat and sauté the onion for 3 to 4 minutes. Add the garlic and sauté for 2 more minutes. Add the poblanos and the chipotles in adobo sauce and continue to cook, stirring, until the peppers are tender, 3 to 5 minutes.

• Stir in the tomato paste and mix well. Add the honey, 2/3 cup (150 mL) orange juice, brown sugar, vinegar, Worcestershire, and liquid smoke. Stir to combine and bring to a boil.

• Lower heat to a simmer for 10 to 15 minutes, stirring occasionally to avoid burning. If sauce becomes too thick, thin with a small amount of orange juice. Remove from heat and allow to cool slightly.

• Pour sauce into a blender. Process until smooth and then transfer to a storage container. Sauce will keep, refrigerated, for 7 to 10 days.

• Preheat grill to high (500ºF/260ºC).

• Remove ribs from the marinade, reserving some of the marinade.

• Sear the rib pieces for 3 to 4 minutes a side.

• Turn off the right-hand burner. Set the smoker tube on the left-hand burner. Place the ribs on the right-hand, "cool" burner. Close the lid.

• Adjust the heat on the left-hand burner to maintain 325ºF (165ºC). Smoke-grill the ribs for 2 to 2½ hours, or until very tender, replacing the wood chips in the tube and basting the ribs with the reserved marinade a few times. Try not to leave the lid open for more time than absolutely necessary to minimize fluctuations in the heat.

• When ribs are tender, turn heat up to medium-high (450ºF/230ºC). Finish ribs by grilling over medium-high heat for 8 to 10 minutes a side, brushing with the sauce.

• Place ribs on a large platter and drizzle more sauce over them. Serve.

TIP: Beef ribs are growing in popularity and unfortunately price. But they are still a great and delicious bargain. They are always available in large Asian supermarkets but be sure to tell them you don't want them cut or they'll be in the saw being turned into short ribs before you can say boo. If you've cultivated your butcher you can get a full rack fairly easily but they usually split them into single ribs for sale. If you can only buy them that way that's fine. Beef ribs are usually very meaty and when slow cooked extremely tender and flavourful. Your dog will love the leftovers.

COOKING BEEF
THE SIZZLE ZONE™ WAY

INFRARED COOKING

Infrared energy is a form of electromagnetic energy with a wavelength just greater than the red end of the visible light spectrum but lower than that of radio waves. Put more simply, it's the main form of energy the sun uses to warm the earth, as Sir William Herschel discovered in 1800. Infrared rays travel through the vacuum of space and penetrate various materials, such as our skin, increasing molecular activity, which creates internal friction. We feel this as warmth.

Foods cooked over infrared heat sources follow this same principle. Charcoal provides the traditional infrared cooking that we're all familiar with. Glowing briquettes radiate intense heat, cooking foods quickly with little moisture loss. The fats and juices that do fall away hit the charcoal and vaporize instantly, passing that delicious smoky flavour back up to the food.

The Napoleon® SIZZLE ZONE™ uses ceramic burners with thousands of evenly spaced flame ports to generate infrared radiant energy. The flames' energy is absorbed by the ceramics, which then glow and heat up to as high as 1800ºF (985ºC). The intensity of this SIZZLE ZONE™ heat quickly sears your meat, locking in the moisture and flavour. The result is unmistakeably succulent and flavourful food in a much reduced grill time, without the hassle or mess of charcoal. The SIZZLE ZONE™ also provides a much more consistent and easily regulated heat source. In other words, the whole cooking surface is consistently hot. The burners can be set very high for rapid searing and cooking perfect steaks and burgers, or turned lower after searing for slightly slower cooking.

Traditional gas burners heat food differently. The air around the burner is heated by combustion and rises up to cook the food at lower temperatures ideally suited to more delicate foods or those you want to slow-cook over time. Napoleon® grills are ideally suited to such combination cooking as searing a delectable prime rib roast over the high heat of the infrared burner and then slow roasting over the traditional burners, either directly or indirectly. The result is a delicious, seasoned crusty exterior and a gush of rich, meaty juices when you cut into the roast.

This infrared technology that provides such great retention of moisture and flavour requires very little preheat time. Since the radiant energy is delivered directly to the food so quickly there is very little heat transferred to the air around the grill. The food cooks quickly, losing far less weight in the process. Of course this also means less fuel is used. If you are a winter griller this SIZZLE ZONE™ is especially handy, since in cold weather propane and gas do not flow as readily, making it difficult to maintain pressure for consistent heat on traditional burners.

Infrared cooking is about twice as fast as traditional grilling. A steak is ready in less than 5 minutes. It's a simple matter of the relationship between food, heat, and time. There are virtually no flare-ups since drippings instantly vaporize. Use the infrared burner for steak, seafood — even vegetables.

Like every new cooking method, practise makes perfect. In this section we provide you with some basic recipes to get you comfortable with this concept and throughout this book there are various references to using the infrared burners. We encourage you to try this very special way to cook.

The basic infrared method is:

1. Preheat.
2. Sear.
3. Turn down to finish.
4. Remove and rest.
5. Bon appétit!

TIPS:

- Meat should be fully thawed, and excess fat trimmed.

- Vegetables and fruit should be cut in uniform and fairly large pieces.

- With seafood and vegetables, as well as lean meats, spray or brush both sides with oil.

- As a general rule, expect your cooking times to be cut in half compared to cooking over traditional gas burners.

THE BASIC GUIDE TO COOKING A PERFECT INFRARED STEAK

1. Choose your steak. Buy the best quality you can afford. I like a rib steak, bone on and about 1¼ to 1¾ inches (3 to 4 cm) thick. Look for even marbling with no big clumps of fat and no more than ¼ inch (0.5 cm) of fat around the outside.

The tender cuts do the best with this rapid high-heat method. We suggest these steaks as good choices for your perfect infrared results: beef tenderloin steaks, filet mignon, rib steak, bone on or off, T-bone, porterhouse and strip loin.

2. About 30 minutes before you want to eat, take the steak(s) out of the refrigerator and remove any wrapping or packaging. Pat dry with paper towels. Season both sides with your favourite seasoning or use coarse salt, freshly ground black pepper, and granulated garlic. Massage into the meat. Let sit to come to room temperature.

3. Preheat the infrared burner for 1 minute to medium-high (you shouldn't be able to hold your hand 3 inches/7.5 cm from the grid for more than 1 or 2 seconds).

4. Place seasoned steak on grid (lid up or down).

5. Wait 2 minutes, then turn steak with tongs. Note: Don't use any tool, such as a fork, that will pierce the meat and cause you to lose the quickly sealed juices.

6. Wait another 2 minutes. Turn off the burner.

7. Dress your baked potato while your steak rests for 1 to 2 minutes.

8. Enjoy your perfect medium-rare steak.

THE ROTISSERIE

The infrared rotisserie burner on the back of the grill will sear the meat evenly on all sides and do a really amazing job of giving you a juicy and deliciously flavoured product.

- If the food is not turning properly, it will not cook evenly. When you begin, watch carefully and adjust if it's not turning smoothly.

- The maximum weight the rotisserie will hold is 15 lb (7 kg). A 15-lb unstuffed turkey should be your reasonable limit.

- If you are tying a roast or trussing a bird, be sure to use cotton twine. Nylon or plastic will melt.

- Place a pan under the roast to catch drippings. Use those drippings.

- Keep the lid closed while rotisserie is cooking unless a recipe specifically tells you to leave it open. This concentrates the heat, locking in the juices and speeding up the cooking time.

- Reserve any basting to the final 30 to 40 minutes of the cooking time to prevent sugars browning too quickly and burning.

- Most tender cuts of meat that roast well will benefit from the rotisserie. Many of your favourite recipes will adapt well.

- Napoleon® has additional accessories like the Tumble Basket and the Rotary Shish Kebab. If you've invested in the rotisserie, consider an adventure with these toys as well.

- The length of time it takes to cook on the infrared rotisserie depends on many factors. We provide a chart of approximate times to give you a starting point. As you become experienced with your grill, you will become your own rotisserie master.

GRILLING MEAT WITH INFRARED

(Times may vary slightly. Insure meats are fully thawed before grilling.)

Infrared Meat	Thickness	Sear Side 1	Sear Side 2	Finish Side 1	Finish Side 2
Hamburger	5/8"	HI - 2 min 30 sec	HI - 2 min 30 sec	HI - 1 min	HI - 1 min
Sprinkle with Napoleon® Creole Cajun Spice on both sides					
Filet Mignon	1 3/8"	HI - 2 min 30 sec	HI - 2 min 30 sec	MED - LOW - 5 min	MED - LOW - 5 min
Apply Napoleon® Classic Steak Spice to both sides. Medium rare is superb					
Top Sirloin	1"	HI - 2 min 30 sec	HI - 2 min 30 sec	MED - LOW - 3 min	MED - LOW - 3 min
Rub with Napoleon® Country Herb or Classic Steak Spice or after cooking baste in Napoleon® Amazing Steak Sauce					
Boneless Pork Chop	5/8"	HI - 2 min	HI - 2 min	HI - 3 min	HI - 3 min
Baste with Napoleon's Mango BBQ Sauce					
Pork Baby Back Ribs	N/A	HI - 2 min	HI - 2 min	MED - LOW - 1 min 30 sec	MED - LOW - 1 min 30 sec
Place ribs and your favourite marinade in a bag. Refrigerate overnight. Brush with Napoleon's Fire Roasted Garlic Sauce before grilling					
Chicken Breasts Boneless, Skinless Thick	1 1/4"	HI - 2 min	HI - 2 min	LOW - 6 min	LOW - 6 min
Trim excess fat. Use marinade or Napoleon® Spice rub of choice - try Napoleon® Chicken & Rib Spice					
Salmon Fillet	3/4"	HI - 2 min	MED-6 min-skin side	N/A	N/A
Spray with non-stick cooking oil on both sides. Try Napoleon's Peanut Satay Sauce					
Halibut	1 1/2"	HI - 2 min 30 sec	HI - 2 min 30 sec	MED - LOW - 3 min 30 sec	MED - LOW - 3 min 30 sec
Use a lemon-herb seasoning. Spray with non-stick cooking oil on both sides					

GRILLING VEGETABLES WITH INFRARED

Vegetable	Sear Side 1	Sear Side 2	Finish Side 1	Finish Side 2
Zucchini	HI - 1 min 50 sec	HI - 1 min 50 sec	N/A	N/A
Cut off stem. Cut into 1/4" thick slices. Spray with non-stick cooking oil on both sides and sprinkle with garlic salt. Finish on warming rack for 3-4 min				
Asparagus	HI - 1 min	HI - 1 min	N/A	N/A
Blanch in boiling water for 1 minute. Remove from boiling water and immediately immerse in bowl of ice water until asparagus has cooled. Dry asparagus on paper towel. Coat with olive oil; salt and pepper. *Finish on warming rack. Remove when tender but slightly firm				
Corn On The Cob In Husk	N/A	N/A	LOW - 12 min Turn every 2 minutes	N/A
Soak whole cob in cold water for 5-10 minutes. Grill corn in husk directly on cooking grids. *Rotate corn 1/4 turn every 2 minutes to ensure even grilling				

VEAL AND LAMB

VEAL RIB CHOPS
WITH GREEN MANGO SALAD AND PINK LADY BARBECUE SAUCE

GREEN MANGO SALAD

4	medium green mangoes, peeled and cut in 1-inch (2.5 cm) pieces	4
2	bunches watercress, stems removed	2
2 tbsp	thinly sliced lime zest	30 mL
1	small red onion, halved and sliced thinly lengthwise	1

PINK LADY BARBECUE SAUCE

1 cup	pink lemonade	250 mL
1 tsp	fresh ginger, peeled and grated	5 mL
½ cup	whole canned lychees, drained	125 mL
½ cup	lychee syrup (from can)	125 mL
¼ cup	rice vinegar	60 mL
1 tbsp	mirin (sweet rice wine), or dry sherry	15 mL
¼ cup	Thai sweet chile sauce	60 mL
1 tsp	grenadine syrup	5 mL
1 tsp	pink peppercorns	5 mL
	Salt and freshly ground black pepper	
6	bone-in veal rib chops (about 14 oz/400 g each), 1¼ inch (3 cm) thick	6
3 tbsp	Garlic and Herb Rub (see recipe, page 26)	45 mL

GREEN MANGO SALAD: In a bowl, combine the mango, watercress, lime zest, and red onion. Toss and set aside.

PINK LADY BARBECUE SAUCE: Whisk together the lemonade, ginger, lychee syrup, vinegar, rice wine, chilli sauce, grenadine, and pink peppercorns. Set aside ½ cup (125 mL) of the sauce at this point. Stir the whole lychees into the rest of the sauce and season with salt and pepper. Set aside at room temperature.

• Pat the chops dry with paper towels and massage the Garlic and Herb Rub into both sides of the meat, pressing so the seasoning adheres well. Let sit for 30 to 45 minutes at room temperature.

• Preheat the grill to high (500°F/260°C).

• Sear the chops for 2 to 3 minutes on each side, or until nicely browned. Reduce the heat to medium (350°F/175°C). Close the lid and grill-roast for 3 to 5 minutes a side, or to an internal temperature of 135°F (57°C). Veal should not be cooked more than medium, as it will become extremely dry and unpalatable.

• Remove from the grill and let rest, loosely covered, for 5 minutes.

• Toss the mango salad with the reserved sauce and place on individual plates. Set the chops to slightly overlap on the salad and drizzle with the Pink Lady Barbecue Sauce.

Serves 4 to 6
Prep Time: 1 hour
Marinade Time: 45 minutes
Cook Time: 15 minutes

ROAST LEG OF LAMB
WITH ROSEMARY, GARLIC, AND LEMON

1	recipe Garlic and Herb Rub (see recipe, page 26)	1
2 tbsp	fresh rosemary, chopped	30 mL
1 tbsp	fresh thyme, chopped	15 mL
2 tsp	freshly cracked black pepper	10 mL
1 tbsp	kosher salt	15 mL
2 tbsp	Dijon mustard	30 mL
2 tbsp	lemon zest, chopped finely	30 mL
2 tbsp	freshly squeezed lemon juice	30 mL
1	fresh bone-in lamb leg (about 8 lbs/4 kg)	1
1	lemon, zested and juiced	1

• In a small nonreactive bowl, combine the Garlic and Herb Rub, rosemary, thyme, pepper, salt, mustard, lemon zest, and lemon juice and stir well.

• Pat the leg of lamb dry with paper towels and trim of any excess clumps of fat. Rub the leg all over with the garlic-herb mixture, massaging it into all the creases and crevasses and patting to make it adhere in a sort of coat. Place the leg in a roasting pan and let it sit for 1 hour at room temperature.

• Preheat the grill to high (500°F/260°C).

• Set the lamb leg on the preheated grill and sear on all sides until nicely browned, about 3 minutes a surface.

• Reduce the heat to medium (350°F/175°C). Close the lid and grill the lamb for about 10 to 12 minutes a side, or until a thermometer inserted without contacting the bone reads 130°F (54°C) for medium-rare.

• Remove from the grill, loosely cover with foil, and let rest for 10 to 15 minutes.

• Carve from the bone and serve immediately.

Serves 6 to 8
Prep Time: 15 minutes
Marinade Time: 1 hour
Cook Time: 25 minutes

PERFECT RACK OF LAMB
WITH MUSTARD GLAZE

¼ cup	soft butter	60 mL
2	cloves garlic, minced	2
2 tbsp	fresh parsley, chopped	30 mL
1 tbsp	fresh marjoram, chopped	15 mL
1 tbsp	fresh rosemary, chopped	15 mL
⅔ cup	fresh bread crumbs	150 mL
½ cup	Dijon mustard	125 mL
3	lamb racks, 7 to 8 bones each, (ask your butcher to trim excess fat and trim (French) the bones) Salt and freshly ground black pepper to taste	3

• In a flat dish, combine the butter, garlic, parsley, marjoram, rosemary, and bread crumbs and mix well.

• Put the Dijon mustard in a small bowl.

• Place the crumb mixture, mustard, a pair of tongs, and a basting brush beside the grill.

• Preheat one side of the grill to high (500°F/260°C).

• With a sharp knife, lightly score a diamond pattern through the fat on the meat side of the racks, trying not to pierce the meat. Lay the racks, meat side down, over the hot side of the grill to sear. Keep the bones away from the heat and leave to form a nice deep brown crust, about 5 to 7 minutes. Do not allow racks to burn. If they are browning too quickly, move them away from the direct heat for a moment.

• Using tongs, lift each rack by the bones and brush seared meat with a layer of Dijon mustard, then dip into the crumb mixture and press down so a thick coat of the mix will adhere.

• Set the coated racks, bone side down, on the cool side of the grill, near the heat, but with the rib ends pointing away from the lit side. Close the lid and roast until crust has browned and the rack is medium-rare to medium, 130°F to 135°F (54°C to 57°C), about 15 to 20 minutes.

• Remove the racks to a platter. Allow to rest, uncovered (so crumb coat doesn't get soggy), for 3 to 5 minutes.

• Carve the racks between every 1 or 2 bones. Arrange on a platter or cluster bones together to form an attractive pile on individual plates. Serve immediately.

Serves 4 to 6
Prep Time: 30 minutes
Cook Time: 25 minutes

PORK

ABOUT RIBS

SPARERIBS are cut from the side where they attach to the breastbone of the pig. They will commonly have rib cartilage and split breastbone attached. The cartilage is not really edible and is best removed. The flap of meat that runs from the breast down to the last three ribs can be left on or trimmed and cooked separately. These ribs are very meaty as well as fatty, but, when cooked properly, very flavourful. The heavy fat over the last three ribs should be trimmed, but since this cut needs long slow cooking, the fat on the rest of the ribs helps give a moist, tender result. Retail spareribs will commonly weigh about 2½ to 3½ pounds (1.1 to 1.5 kg).

BABY BACK RIBS are made up of the strip of rib bones obtained when boning the entire loin. Button bones should be trimmed, and this cut will not contain any of the backbone. They are more expensive since they contain loin and tenderloin meat. They are less fatty than spareribs and they have a larger meat-to-bone ratio. Chefs will tell you these are their favourite eating ribs every time.

COUNTRY-STYLE RIBS are very meaty. This cut comes from the rib end of the pork loin, usually with only a few bones attached. They are cheaper than spareribs and back ribs and require a long cooking time but are well worth the extra effort.

PORK BACK RIB TAIL PIECES are not easy to find, but occasionally you will see them offered in bags labelled Ribbits or Rib Tips or Rib Tail. They are 6- to 8-inch (15 to 20 cm) long, meaty pieces cut from the end of the baby back rib and can be a very satisfying purchase.

COOKING RIBS

Ribs can be boiled, steamed, and oven roasted with great results. But we are concerned with the grill. Our recipes will give you the "how to" for grilling and smoking.

GRILLING — Low heat, patience, and desire are the principles of grilling perfect ribs. You'll notice we recommend maintaining heat no higher than 325ºF (165ºC) and adding moisture via a drip pan. We marinate and we rub, but don't add sauce until close to the end so there's no burnt bits, just tender, sweet, flavourful meat falling from the bones. Spareribs will take about 90 minutes; back and country style slightly less.

SMOKING — The heat is even lower (225ºF/110ºC). The time is even longer. The results are glorious. Get familiar with the wood chips you have available to you, and use the Napoleon® Smoker Tube. Again, there will be marinating and rubbing, and there will also be wood chips to smoke. Expect spareribs to take 3 to 4 hours. Back and country-style ribs will take about 3. You'll boost the heat at the end for maybe 10 minutes to give a final glaze of sauce.

Once you master our recipes, you're ready to create your own!

BEER-BASTED, GRILL-SMOKED ST. LOUIS RIBS

1 bag Napoleon® Smoker Wood Chips
(hickory or alder)
Napoleon® Smoker Tube

4	racks St. Louis style ribs (about 2½ lbs/1.1 kg each)	4
1	recipe Beer Marinade (see recipe, page 30)	1
½ cup	Rib and Chicken BBQ Seasoning and Rub (see recipe, page 17)	125 mL
1 cup	Gourmet-Style Barbecue Sauce (see recipe, page 44)	250 mL

A common cut of spareribs is named for the town of St. Louis. Basically, the breastbone and skirt are removed and the ribs are cut lengthwise to form a uniform rectangle with all the bones the same length.

• Work a sharp knife under the membrane on the back side of the ribs. Once you have a piece large enough, use a paper towel to get a good grip. Gently pull the membrane away from the ribs. The marinade and seasoning will not penetrate this membrane and the ribs will curl as they cook if the membrane is not removed or scored. Place the ribs in a roasting pan.

• Pour the marinade over the ribs. Cover and marinate for at least 4 to 6 hours or overnight. Place the wood chips in water to soak while the ribs are marinating.

• Preheat the grill to low (225ºF/110ºC).

• Remove the ribs from the marinade, reserving the marinade for basting, and rub, massaging well, with the Rib and Chicken BBQ Seasoning and Rub.

• Place the soaked Napoleon® Smoker Wood Chips in the tube and place over the preheated left side of the grill. Turn off the right side of the grill.

• Place the ribs on the right side of the grill (indirect heat) and close the lid. Baste with the reserved marinade every hour and replenish the smoker chips with fresh soaked chips several times for maximum flavour. After 3½ to 4½ hours, ribs will be tender and bones will wiggle a little when pulled.

• Turn both sides of grill up to medium-high (450ºF/230ºC). Grill smoked ribs for 8 to 10 minutes a side, brushing liberally with the Gourmet-Style Barbecue Sauce or your favourite barbecue sauce.

• Cut racks in halves or thirds and serve on a large platter with more sauce on the side.

Serves 4 to 8
Prep Time: 45 minutes
Marinade Time: 4 hours to overnight
Cook Time: 5 hours

TIP: Bone-in cuts of meat such as ribs or chicken breasts should always be started bone side down on the grill.

SHIRAZ SMOKED BABY BACK RIBS

Napoleon® Smoker Wood Chips (cherry or apple), soaked for 2 hours
Napoleon® Smoker Tube

4	racks pork baby back ribs	4
3 cups	Shiraz	750 mL
1 cup	water	250 mL
½ cup	granulated sugar	125 mL
¼ cup	salt	60 mL
¼ cup	Cajun Creole Seasoning and Rub (see recipe, page 17)	60 mL

SAUCE

2 tbsp	vegetable oil	30 mL
1	small onion, finely diced	1
4	cloves garlic, minced	4
1 cup	Grill-Roasted Garlic Barbecue Sauce (see recipe, page 47)	250 mL
½ cup	Shiraz	125 mL
½ cup	liquid honey	125 mL
¼ cup	grape jelly	60 mL
¼ tsp	cayenne pepper, or to taste	1 mL
	Freshly ground black pepper and salt	

• Work a sharp knife under the membrane on the back side of the ribs. Once you have a piece large enough, use a paper towel to get a good grip. Gently pull the membrane away from the ribs. The marinade and seasoning will not penetrate this membrane and the ribs will curl as they cook if the membrane is not removed or scored. Place the ribs in a roasting pan.

• Combine the 3 cups (750 mL) Shiraz, water, sugar, and salt. Stir to dissolve sugar and salt, then pour over the ribs. Cover and marinate for at least 4 hours or overnight.

• Preheat the grill to low (225ºF/110ºC).

• Remove the ribs from the marinade, reserving the marinade for basting, and rub, massaging well, with Cajun Creole Seasoning and Rub.

• Place the soaked Napoleon® Smoker Wood Chips in the tube over the preheated left side of the grill. Turn off the right side of the grill.

• Place the ribs over the right side of the grill (indirect heat) and close the lid. Baste with the reserved marinade every hour and replenish the smoker chips with fresh soaked chips several times for maximum flavour. After 3 to 3½ hours, ribs will be tender and bones will wiggle a little when pulled.

SAUCE: While ribs are smoking, prepare sauce. In a medium saucepan, heat oil and sauté onion and garlic for 2 to 3 minutes. Add Grill-Roasted Garlic Barbecue Sauce, the ½ cup (125 mL) Shiraz, honey, and grape jelly and bring to a boil, whisking to combine. Reduce heat and simmer for 10 to 15 minutes, stirring occasionally. Season to taste with cayenne, black pepper, and salt. Remove from heat.

• Turn both sides of grill up to medium-high (450ºF/230ºC). Grill smoked ribs for 10 to 12 minutes a side, basting liberally with sauce.

• Cut between every third rib and serve.

Serves 4 to 6
Prep Time: 45 minutes
Marinade Time: 4 hours to overnight
Cook Time: 4 hours

GRILLED BABY BACK RIBS
WITH HONEY MUSTARD AND BROWN SUGAR RUB

Napoleon® Rib Rack and Pan

HONEY MUSTARD

½ cup	spicy brown mustard	125 mL
½ cup	firmly packed dark brown sugar	125 mL
¼ cup	honey	60 mL
¼ cup	white wine vinegar	60 mL

BROWN SUGAR RUB

1 cup	firmly packed dark brown sugar	250 mL
¼ cup	granulated garlic	60 mL
¼ cup	Rib and Chicken BBQ Seasoning and Rub (see recipe, page 17)	60 mL
2 tbsp	onion salt	30 mL
2 tbsp	celery salt	30 mL
2 tbsp	freshly ground black pepper	30 mL
2 tbsp	rubbed sage	30 mL
2 tsp	dried rosemary	10 mL
1 tsp	dried thyme	5 mL
4	racks Baby Back Ribs	4
1 cup	Hof Brau Barbecue Sauce (see recipe, page 47)	250 mL

HONEY MUSTARD: In a nonreactive bowl, whisk together the mustard, ½ cup (125 mL) brown sugar, honey, and vinegar and set aside.

BROWN SUGAR RUB: Combine the 1 cup (250 mL) brown sugar, garlic, Rib and Chicken BBQ Seasoning and Rub, onion salt, celery salt, pepper, sage, rosemary, and thyme and mix well.

• Work a sharp knife under the membrane on the back side of the ribs. Once you have a piece large enough, use a paper towel to get a good grip. Gently pull the membrane away from the ribs. Trim away any large pieces of fat.

• Brush the Honey Mustard over the ribs. Rub the slathered ribs with the Brown Sugar Rub and set the ribs in a pan to sit for 30 minutes before grilling.

• Preheat the grill to 325ºF (165ºC). Turn off the right side and set a drip pan under the grate.

• Place the ribs in the Napoleon® Rib Rack and place the rack over the drip pan (or place the ribs, bone side down, directly on the grate over the drip pan). Close the lid and cook for 1½ to 2 hours, or until bones wiggle easily when pulled. During the last 10 to 15 minutes, brush the ribs lightly with Hof Brau sauce.

• Serve racks with Hof Brau Sauce on the side for dipping.

Serves 4 to 6
Prep Time: 45 minutes
Marinade Time: 30 minutes
Cook Time: 2 hours

BRAISED ST. LOUIS RIBS
WITH CHERRY COLA BARBECUE SAUCE

MARINADE

3 cups	cherry cola	750 mL
½ cup	cider vinegar	125 mL
½ cup	soy sauce	125 mL
2 tbsp	pureed garlic	30 mL
2 cups	water	500 mL
4	racks St. Louis style ribs (about 2¼ lb/1 kg each)	4
¼ cup	Kansas City Rub (see recipe, page 25)	60 mL

CHERRY COLA BARBECUE SAUCE

1 tbsp	olive oil	15 mL
1	small onion, finely diced	1
3	cloves garlic, minced	3
1 tsp	chili powder	5 mL
1 tsp	ground cumin	5 mL
1⅓ cups	ketchup	325 mL
⅔ cup	cherry cola	150 mL
¼ cup	soy sauce	60 mL
¼ cup	cider vinegar	60 mL
1	drop liquid smoke	1
	Freshly ground black pepper to taste	

MARINADE: Combine the 2 cans of cherry cola, ½ cup (125 mL) vinegar, ½ cup (125 mL) soy sauce, puréed garlic, and water and mix well.

• Work a sharp knife under the membrane on the back side of the ribs. Once you have a piece large enough, use a paper towel to get a good grip. Gently pull the membrane away from the ribs. Trim away any large pieces of fat.

• Place ribs in a roasting pan and pour the marinade over. Cover and marinate in the refrigerator for 4 to 6 hours or overnight.

• Preheat oven to 325ºF (165ºC).

• Pour all but 2 cups (500 mL) of the marinade off the ribs. Cover the roasting pan tightly, either with a lid or with foil. Braise in the preheated oven for 2 to 2½ hours, or until tender. Allow to cool enough to be handled.

CHERRY COLA BARBECUE SAUCE: While ribs are braising, make the sauce. In a saucepan, heat the olive oil over medium heat. Sauté the onions for 4 to 5 minutes without allowing to brown. Add minced garlic and continue cooking for 2 minutes. Stir in the chili powder and cumin and continue stirring for 1 to 2 minutes. Stir in the ketchup, the ⅔ cup (325 mL) cherry cola, ¼ cup (60 mL) soy sauce, ¼ cup (60 mL) vinegar, and liquid smoke. Season with pepper. Simmer for 5 minutes. Remove from the heat.

• Preheat the grill to medium-high (450ºF/230ºC).

• Grill ribs for 10 to 12 minutes a side, basting liberally with the sauce.

• Cut between every third rib and serve.

Serves 4 to 6
Prep Time: 45 minutes
Marinade Time: 4 hours to overnight
Cook Time: 3½ hours

DOUBLE-THICK TANDOORI PORK CHOPS
WITH RAITA

Napoleon® Meat Injector

INJECTOR SEASONING

5 tbsp	melted butter	75 mL
2 tbsp	malt vinegar	30 mL
½ cup	Tandoori Marinade (see recipe, page 29)	125 mL
6	boneless pork loin chops, (about 8 oz/ 250 g each), about 3 inches (7.5 cm) thick	6
¼ cup	Tandoori Seasoning and Rub (see recipe, page 21)	60 mL

SAUCE

2 tbsp	unsalted butter	30 mL
3	cloves garlic, minced	3
1	small onion, finely diced	1
½ cup	firmly packed brown sugar	125 mL
¼ cup	liquid honey	60 mL
2 tbsp	malt vinegar	30 mL
2 tbsp	soy sauce	30 mL
½ cup	Tandoori Marinade (see recipe, page 29)	125 mL

RAITA

2 cups	plain yogurt	500 mL
¾ cup	cucumber, not English peeled, seeded, and coarsely grated	180 mL
1	small onion, coarsely grated	1
2 tsp	fresh chopped cilantro	10 mL
2 tsp	sugar	10 mL
1 tbsp	fresh squeezed lemon juice sea salt to taste	15 mL

INJECTOR SEASONING: In a saucepan over low heat, combine the melted butter, 2 tbsp (30 mL) vinegar, and ½ cup (125 mL) Tandoori Marinade.

• Using the Napoleon® Injector, inject each chop in the centre with about 3 tbsp (45 mL) of the mixture. Rub the chops with the Tandoori Rub, massaging into the meat. Cover and refrigerate if not grilling within 30 minutes.

SAUCE: In another saucepan, melt the 2 tbsp (30 mL) butter over medium-high heat and sauté garlic and onions for 2 to 3 minutes. Add brown sugar, honey, the 2 tbsp (30 mL) vinegar, and soy sauce and bring to a boil. Simmer, stirring occasionally, for 10 minutes. Remove from heat and whisk in the ½ cup (125 mL) Tandoori Marinade. Set aside.

• Preheat grill to high (500ºF/260ºC).

• Sear chops for 1 to 2 minutes on each side. Reduce heat to medium (350ºF/175ºC) and close lid. Slow-roast for 12 to 15 minutes, basting occasionally with the sauce, until just cooked through and juices run clear. For medium, the internal temperature should be 145ºF (63ºC) before a 5-minute rest.

• Drizzle with sauce and serve with more sauce on the side.

RAITA: Combine all ingredients and mix well. Cover and refrigerate until needed.

Serves 6
Prep Time: 30 minutes
Marinade Time: 30 minutes
Cook Time: 20 minutes

GRILLED PORK CHOPS
WITH GRILLED PINEAPPLE BARBECUE SAUCE

2 tbsp	ground cinnamon	30 mL
1 tbsp	granulated sugar	15 mL
1 tbsp	ground cumin	15 mL
1 tbsp	ground allspice	15 mL
2 tsp	ground ginger	10 mL
2 tsp	granulated garlic	10 mL
2 tsp	salt	10 mL
3 cups	dark beer	750 mL
¼ cup	firmly packed brown sugar	60 mL
1 tbsp	salt	15 mL
6	pork loin chops (about 6 oz/175 g each), 1 inch (2.5 cm) thick	6

GRILLED PINEAPPLE BARBECUE SAUCE

¼ cup	vegetable oil, divided	60 mL
1	pineapple, peeled and sliced into ½-inch (1 cm) thick rounds	1
	Salt and freshly ground black pepper to taste	
1	small onion, finely diced	1
3	cloves garlic, minced	3
3 cups	Kansas City Barbecue Sauce (with liquid smoke; see recipe, page 39)	750 mL
½ cup	firmly packed brown sugar	125 mL
½ cup	bourbon	125 mL
¼ cup	Dijon mustard	60 mL

Serves 6
Prep Time: 45 minutes
Marinade Time: 12 to 24 hours
Cook Time: 10 minutes

TIP: To stop chops or steaks from curling up, use a sharp knife to make a few slits in the fat around the edge.

• Combine the cinnamon, sugar, cumin, allspice, ginger, garlic, and 2 tsp (10 mL) salt and mix well.

• Rub the chops with the seasoning mixture, massaging well to work the seasoning into the flesh.

• Whisk together the beer, ¼ cup (60 mL) brown sugar, and 1 tbsp (15 mL) salt to combine and to dissolve the sugar and salt.

• Place the chops in a dish large enough to hold them in a single layer. Pour the marinade over, turning the chops to coat. Cover and refrigerate for 12 to 24 hours.

• Preheat the grill to medium-high (450ºF/230ºC).

GRILLED PINEAPPLE BARBECUE SAUCE: Rub 2 tbsp (30 mL) of the oil all over the pineapple rounds and season them with salt and pepper. Grill for 3 to 4 minutes a side, or until golden brown, tender, and lightly charred. Cool and cut into ¼-inch (0.5 cm) cubes, discarding the tough core.

• In a large saucepan, heat the remaining 2 tbsp (30 mL) oil. Add the onions and garlic and sauté for 3 to 4 minutes, until tender and fragrant. Stir in the barbecue sauce, ½ cup (125 mL) brown sugar, bourbon, and mustard. Bring slowly to a boil, stirring constantly.

• Stir in the pineapple and simmer for 5 minutes. Remove from the heat and set aside.

• Preheat the grill to medium-high (450ºF/230ºC).

• Remove the chops from the marinade. Discard the marinade. Grill the chops on one side for 4 to 5 minutes. Turn and grill for another 5 to 6 minutes, basting with the pineapple sauce. Chops are done when juices run clear and/or internal temperature reaches 145ºF (63ºC). Let rest 3 to 4 minutes before serving.

• Serve with warm pineapple sauce drizzled over.

TIP: Contrary to old beliefs pork does not need to be cooked to death to be safe. If you have an internal temperature of 145ºF (63ºC) when you remove a piece of pork from the grill, you will have 150ºF (66ºC) or more after 3 to 4 minutes of rest. This is a perfect medium. When you cut into it there will be the very faintest tinge of pink, and clear juices will run.

BACON-WRAPPED PORK STEAKS
WITH APPLE CIDER SAUCE AND PLANK-GRILLED APPLES

untreated Napoleon® 12-inch cedar plank,
soaked for 12 hours

APPLE CIDER SAUCE

2 cups	apple cider	500 mL
1 cup	liquid honey	250 mL
½ cup	soy sauce	125 mL
2 tbsp	freshly cracked black pepper	30 mL
2 tbsp	fresh cilantro, chopped	30 mL
8	cloves garlic, minced	8
1	medium onion, thinly sliced	1
5	green onions, thinly sliced	5
6	pork shoulder butt steaks (about 8 oz/227 g each), 1½ inches (4 cm) thick	6
	Salt to taste	
12	slices thick-cut bacon	12
6	baking apples, such as Cortland or Granny Smith	6
¼ cup	butter, softened	60 mL
¼ cup	firmly packed brown sugar	180 mL

APPLE CIDER SAUCE: Stir together the cider, honey, soy sauce, pepper, cilantro, garlic, sliced onion, and green onions.

• Place the steaks in a glass dish large enough to hold them in a single layer. Pour enough marinade over the steaks to cover, reserving any sauce that's not used. Cover and refrigerate for 4 to 6 hours.

• Remove the steaks from the marinade and pour the marinade, plus any reserved, into a saucepan. Bring the marinade to a boil and continue boiling until reduced by half. Use a hand-held blender or pour into a standard blender and purée the sauce until smooth.

• Wrap 2 slices of bacon around each pork steak, securing with a toothpick.

• Using a melon baller, scoop out the cores of the apples, leaving about an inch (2.5 cm) intact in the bottom to form a closed cavity. Mix together the brown sugar and butter. Pack about 1 tbsp (15 mL) of the butter mixture into the cavities in the apples. Place the apples on the presoaked plank.

• Preheat the grill to medium-high (450°F/230°C).

• Set the plank with the apples on the preheated grill. Drizzle 1 tbsp (15 mL) of sauce into each apple cavity. Close the lid and grill-roast for 30 minutes.

• Open the lid and drizzle 1 tbsp more of the sauce into the apples. Roast for another 10 minutes, or until the apples are tender enough to pierce easily with a toothpick but still hold their shape. Remove from the grill. Cut into 6 to 8 wedges and grill directly over high heat for 1 to 2 minutes per side to lightly char. Remove from grill and keep warm.

• Place steaks on the grill and cook for 5 to 6 minutes a side, basting liberally with the Apple Cider Sauce. Steaks are done when juices run clear, bacon is crisp, and/or internal temperature reaches 145°F (63°C). Let rest 3 to 4 minutes before serving.

• Serve the steaks with a baked apple on the side, drizzling more of the sauce over apple and steak.

Serves 6
Prep Time: 45 minutes
Marinade Time: 4 to 6 hours
Cook Time: 35 minutes

PLANKED PORK AND BEEF MEATLOAF
WITH HERBS AND BEER

untreated Napoleon® 12-inch cedar plank, soaked at least 12 hours

½ lb	ground sirloin beef	250 g
½ lb	ground pork	250 g
¼ cup	Gourmet-Style Barbecue Sauce (see recipe, page 44)	60 mL
1	onion, finely diced	1
3 tbsp	Dijon mustard	45 mL
3	cloves garlic, minced	3
2	green onions, chopped	2
2 tbsp	fresh herbs, chopped (parsley, oregano, thyme, sage, etc.)	30 mL
¼ cup	beer	60 mL
	Salt and freshly ground pepper to taste	
1 lb	sliced bacon	500 g
2 tbsp	Cajun Creole Seasoning and Rub (see recipe, page 17)	30 mL
1 cup	Gourmet-Style Barbecue Sauce (see recipe, page 44)	250 mL
¼ cup	beer	60 mL
	Gourmet-Style Barbecue Sauce for serving	

• In a large bowl, thoroughly combine the ground beef and pork, ¼ cup (60 mL) barbecue sauce, onion, mustard, garlic, green onions, herbs, and ¼ cup (60 mL) beer. Season with salt and pepper.

• Form the meatloaf into a tightly packed oval in the centre of the soaked plank, making sure to leave a 2-inch (5 cm) border around the edge of the plank.

• Wrap slices of bacon around the bottom edge of the loaf to form a border where the loaf meets the plank. Then completely encase the loaf in overlapping bacon slices so that no meatloaf is left exposed.

• Sprinkle with the Cajun Creole Seasoning and Rub. Cover and refrigerate for 1 hour to set the loaf.

• Place the 1 cup (250 mL) of Gourmet Style Barbecue Sauce and ¼ cup (60 mL) beer in a small saucepan on the side burner. Bring to a boil over high heat, then simmer for 4 to 5 minutes to thicken and reduce by half. Remove from the heat and set aside for basting.

• Set a drip pan with ½ inch (1 cm) of water beneath the centre grate of the grill.

• Preheat the grill to medium-high (450°F/230°C).

• Set the planked meatloaf on the centre grate over the drip pan. Close the lid.

• When the plank begins to crackle and smoke, reduce the heat to medium (350°F/175°C). Plank-roast the meatloaf for 35 to 45 minutes with the lid closed, checking occasionally to make sure the plank hasn't ignited. Use a spray bottle of water to keep the edges from flaming.

• Check the meatloaf by inserting a thermometer in the thickest part of the meat. When the internal temperature is 150°F (66°C), baste the meatloaf generously with the sauce-beer mixture. Close the lid for 3 to 5 minutes to allow the sauce to caramelize.

• Using gloves and tongs, remove planked meatloaf from the grill very carefully. It will be hot. Slide it onto a baking sheet or large platter. Cover loosely with foil and let sit for 5 to 7 minutes to rest (to an internal temperature of 165°F/74°C) before cutting in thick slices.

• Serve with Gourmet-Style Barbecue Sauce on the side.

Serves 8
Prep Time: 45 minutes
Cook Time: 50 minutes

JERK ROTISSERIE OF PORK LOIN
WITH MAPLE JERK BARBECUE SAUCE

Napoleon® Meat Injector

1	4½ lb (2 kg) boneless pork loin, about 12–18 (30–45 cm) inches long	1
1	recipe Jerk Marinade (see recipe, page 29), ½ cup (125 mL) reserved for sauce	1
3 cups	beer	750 mL
½ cup	granulated sugar	125 mL
¼ cup	salt	60 mL

MAPLE JERK BBQ SAUCE

½ cup	Jerk Marinade (reserved from above)	60 mL
½ cup	pure maple syrup	125 mL
⅔ cup	beer	150 mL
2½ cups	Mango Barbecue Sauce (see recipe, page 50)	625 mL
	Salt	

• Place the pork loin in a deep roasting pan.

• Whisk together the Jerk Marinade (reserving ½ cup/125 mL for the sauce), 3 cups (750 mL) of beer, sugar, and ¼ cup (60 mL) salt.

• Fill the injector with the seasoning; pierce the pork loin several times and inject directly into the meat. Pour the rest of the marinade over pork loin, cover, and marinate, refrigerated, for 24 hours.

MAPLE JERK BBQ SAUCE: Whisk together the reserved Jerk Marinade, maple syrup, ⅔ cup (150 mL) beer, and Mango Barbecue Sauce.

• Remove pork from the pan and discard the marinade. Skewer with the rotisserie rod, securing the loin with the rotisserie forks as per manufacturer's instructions.

• Preheat infrared burner to high or the barbecue burners to high (500ºF/260ºC).

• Secure the pork onto the rotisserie motor, season with salt, and close the lid. Sear the meat for 15 minutes.

• Reduce infrared burner to medium or burners to medium-low (250ºF/120ºC) and continue to cook for about 1 to 1½ hours, basting frequently with the Maple Jerk BBQ Sauce. Pork should reach a minimum internal temperature of 145ºF/63ºC for medium. Insert a meat thermometer to test, making sure not to touch the rotisserie rod.

• Remove pork from the rotisserie. Using gloves, carefully remove rotisserie rod. Cover meat with foil and let rest for 10 to 15 minutes. Internal Temperature will reach 150ºF/66ºC to 155ºF/68ºC after the rest. Take care not to overcook and dry out the loin.

• Give a final baste and cut into 1-inch (2.5 cm) thick slices. Serve with the Maple Jerk BBQ Sauce on the side.

Serves 6 to 8
Prep Time: 45 minutes
Marinade Time: 24 hours
Cook Time: 2½ hours

PORK SOUVLAKI
WITH TZATZIKI AND GRILLED GARLIC PITAS

8 metal or well-soaked bamboo skewers

3 tbsp	fresh oregano, chopped	45 mL
3 tbsp	kosher or coarse sea salt	45 mL
1½ tbsp	fresh thyme, chopped	22 mL
1½ tbsp	freshly cracked black pepper	22 mL
4	cloves garlic, minced	4
3 tbsp	Greek olive oil	45 mL
2 tbsp	freshly squeezed lemon juice	30 mL
4	whole pork tenderloins (about 1 lb/500 g each), trimmed of any excess fat and silver skin	4

TZATZIKI

2 cups	plain yogurt	500 mL
¾ cup	cucumber (not English), peeled, seeded, finely diced	125 mL
1	small onion, diced finely	1
4	cloves garlic, puréed	4
1 tbsp	fresh dill, chopped	15 mL
1 tbsp	freshly squeezed lemon juice (or more to taste)	15 mL
	Kosher or sea salt and freshly ground black pepper	

GRILLED GARLIC PITAS

3 tbsp	Garlic and Herb Rub (see recipe, page 26)	45 mL
6 tbsp	Greek olive oil	90 mL
12	8-inch (20 cm) fresh pita breads	12
1 lb	haloumi (available at specialty markets) or feta cheese	500 g
	Ripe tomatoes, coarsely chopped	
	Sliced onions	
	Lemon wedges	

• In a large bowl, combine the oregano, salt, thyme, pepper, minced garlic, the 3 tbsp (45 mL) olive oil, and 2 tbsp (30 mL) lemon juice and mix well.

• Pat the tenderloins dry with paper towel. Cut them into 1-inch (2.5 cm) cubes and place them in the bowl with the herb mixture. Toss to thoroughly coat the meat with the herb mix.

• Skewer the cubes, about 6 to 8 cubes a skewer. Set on a baking sheet and drizzle the remaining marinade over. Cover and refrigerate for 1 to 2 hours.

TZATZIKI: Combine the yogurt, cucumber, onion, puréed garlic, dill, and the 1 tbsp (15 mL) lemon juice and mix well. Season with salt and pepper. Cover and refrigerate until needed.

• Preheat the grill to medium-high (450ºF/230ºC).

GRILLED GARLIC PITAS: Combine the Garlic and Herb Rub and the 6 tbsp (90 mL) olive oil. Brush the mixture generously on one side of each pita.

• Grill the skewers for 4 to 5 minutes a side, until cooked to medium (internal temperature of 150ºF/65ºC). Remove from the grill to a platter and cover with foil. Let rest 2 to 3 minutes before serving.

• Place pitas on the grill, brushed side down. Grill briefly to crisp up and heat through.

• Place a pita on a plate, place a souvlaki skewer on the pita, and pull the skewer from the meat. Serve with tzatziki, haloumi or feta, tomatoes, onions, and lemon wedges.

Serves 8
Prep Time: 1 hour
Marinade Time: 1 to 2 hours
Cook Time: 15 minutes

SMOKED PORK
FOR SOUTHERN-STYLE PULLED PORK

Napoleon® Smoker Chips (mesquite, hickory, or
cherry), soaked at least 4 to 6 hours
Napoleon® Smoker Tube

1	lemon, sliced	1
1	large onion, sliced	1
8	cloves garlic, minced	8
2 tbsp	yellow mustard seeds	30 mL
2 tbsp	dry marjoram	30 mL
2 tbsp	kosher salt	30 mL
3 cups	Sprite® (lemon-lime soda)	750 mL
1 cup	water	250 mL
1	pork shoulder roast (4-5 lb/2.2 kg)	1
¼ cup	Hot and Spicy BBQ Seasoning and Rub (see recipe, page 18)	60 mL
3 cups	South Carolina Yellow Mustard Sauce (see recipe, page 43)	750 mL
12	large crusty Italian buns	12

Serves 8 or more
Prep Time: 45 minutes
Marinade Time: 48 hours
Cook Time: 6 hours or more

If you have the patience and fortitude required, this is a delicious dish.

• In a large pot, combine the lemon, onion, garlic, mustard seeds, marjoram, salt, Sprite, and water.

• Submerge the pork roast in the marinade, turning to coat completely. Marinate, covered, in the refrigerator for 24 to 48 hours, turning the roast in the marinade occasionally.

• Remove the roast from the marinade and discard the marinade. Pat the roast lightly with paper towels and then rub with the Hot and Spicy BBQ Seasoning and Rub, massaging well into the meat.

• Preheat grill to high (500ºF/260ºC).

• Turn off the right side. Set the smoker tube on the left-hand burner and a drip pan under the right side. Set the roast on the grate of the right-hand, unlit burner with the drip pan below it. Close the lid.

• Adjust the heat to maintain the grill at no more than 225ºF to 250ºF (107º to 121ºC). Smoke-grill the shoulder for 5 to 6 hours. Every hour or so, replace the wood chips in the smoker tube with fresh soaked chips, but try not to leave the lid open for longer than absolutely necessary, to minimize fluctuations in the heat.

• After 5 to 6 hours, check the roast by inserting a thermometer in the thickest part of the meat. The internal temperature should be 180ºF (82ºC), and when pulled, the blade bone should come cleanly out of the meat.

• Take the roast out of the grill and seal the pan with a double layer of heavy-duty foil. Let it rest for 15 to 20 minutes.

• Remove the crackling (cooked skin) from the roast and slice thinly. Pull the meat from the roast in chunks and shred with a fork or by hand. Place the pork in a large bowl and add South Carolina Mustard Sauce a little at a time, mixing it gently but thoroughly. The amount of sauce is a matter of personal preference.

• The meat should be served piled high on a fresh crusty bun, with Creamy Coleslaw (see recipe, page 118) or Baked Potato Salad with Mustard and Olives (see recipe, page 118) on the side.

TIP: This cannot be rushed. When you hear "low and slow" think pulled pork or brisket.

POULTRY

BEER-CAN CHICKEN

Tallboy (large can; 16 oz/455 mL) beer

2 aluminum pie plates or similar heatproof pan to
    hold chicken

1	chicken (3 to 4 lbs/1.5 to 2 kg)	1
¼ cup	Cajun Creole Seasoning and Rub (see recipe, page 17)	60 mL
¼ cup	butter	60 mL
½ cup	Grill-Roasted Garlic Barbecue Sauce (see recipe, page 47)	125 mL
¼ cup	pure maple syrup	60 mL
1 tbsp	puréed chipotle chile in adobo sauce	15 mL
¼ cup	beer	60 mL

• Preheat the grill to medium-high (450ºF/230ºC).

• Wash the chicken inside and out with cold water and pat dry with paper towels. Rub the chicken inside and out with the Cajun Creole Seasoning and Rub, massaging well and pushing some under the skin directly onto the meat.

BASTING SAUCE: Place the butter, Fire-Roasted Garlic Barbecue Sauce, maple syrup, chipotle pepper, and ¼ cup (60 mL) beer in a small saucepan and heat. Stir to combine. When heated through, set aside.

• Open the tallboy and either take a big sip or pour off about an ounce (30 mL) to leave room for the beer to boil out. Place the beer can on a doubled aluminum pie plate or similar pan. Place the chicken, cavity down, over the can so that the can protrudes far enough into the cavity to stand the bird upright and hold it firmly.

• Place the chicken setup on the preheated grill. Close the lid and roast for 20 minutes a pound, about 60 to 70 minutes, basting liberally, two or three times with the Basting Sauce. Chicken is fully cooked when a thermometer inserted into the thigh registers 160ºF (71ºC).

• With tongs and a large fork, remove the chicken from the beer can very carefully. Both will be very hot and there will be steam. Discard beer and can. Move to a platter and cover loosely with foil. Let rest for 10 minutes.

• Carve the chicken and drizzle pan juices over. Serve with the Basting Sauce on the side.

Serves 4
Prep: 30 minutes
Cook Time: 80 minutes

TUMBLE BASKET CHICKEN THIGHS
WITH WASABI TERIYAKI GLAZE

Napoleon® Tumble Basket

12	skin-on bone-in chicken thighs	12
2 tbsp	Rib and Chicken BBQ Seasoning and Rub (see recipe, page 17)	30 mL

WASABI TERIYAKI GLAZE

2 tbsp	vegetable oil	30 mL
1 tsp	toasted sesame oil	5 mL
4	garlic, minced	4
1 tbsp	finely chopped peeled fresh ginger	15 mL
¼ cup	firmly packed brown sugar	60 mL
¼ cup	rice vinegar	60 mL
½ cup	Mango Barbecue Sauce (see recipe, page 50)	125 mL
¼ cup	soy sauce	60 mL
¼ cup	water	60 mL
1 tbsp	prepared horseradish	15 mL
1 tsp	wasabi powder	5 mL
	Salt and freshly ground pepper to taste	
¼ cup	toasted sesame seeds	60 mL
½ cup	pickled ginger	125 mL

• Sprinkle the chicken thighs with the Rib and Chicken BBQ Seasoning and Rub, patting onto the meat and under the skin.

WASABI TERIYAKI GLAZE: In a medium saucepan, heat the vegetable oil and sesame oil over medium-high heat. Sauté the garlic and ginger for 3 to 4 minutes, until tender and fragrant. Stir in the brown sugar, vinegar, Mango Barbecue Sauce, soy sauce, and water. Bring to a boil and simmer for 10 minutes. Remove from heat and whisk in horseradish and wasabi. Let cool.

• Preheat grill to high (500ºF/260ºC).

• Place thighs in the tumble basket and secure basket to the rotisserie rod as per the manufacturer's instructions. Set the rod on the barbecue, taking care to make sure the basket is firmly held. Place a foil pan directly under the basket to collect drippings. Close the lid and allow chicken thighs to sear over the high heat for 8 to 10 minutes.

• Reduce the heat to medium-high (450ºF/230ºC) and continue cooking for 20 to 30 minutes, basting every 10 to 15 minutes with the glazing sauce. When the thighs are fully cooked, juices will run clear and a meat thermometer will register 165ºF (74ºC). Take care to avoid contact with the bone when checking temperature.

• Remove thighs carefully from the basket — they'll be very hot. Place on a serving platter and baste once more with the glazing sauce.

• Serve sprinkled with the toasted sesame seeds and pickled ginger and more sauce on the side.

Serves 6 to 8
Prep: 30 minutes
Cook Time: 45 minutes

WHOLE ROTISSERIE CHICKEN

1	Foodsafe plastic bag	1
	chicken (3 to 4 lbs/1.5 to 2 kg) or larger	
¼ cup	frozen orange juice concentrate	60 mL
¼ cup	soy sauce	60 mL
¼ cup	freshly squeezed lime juice	60 mL
3 tbsp	fresh cilantro, chopped	45 mL
1 tbsp	toasted sesame oil	15 mL
1 tbsp	minced fresh garlic	15 mL
2 tsp	Jerk Seasoning and Rub (see recipe, page 21)	10 mL
½ tsp	freshly ground black pepper	2 mL
1½ cups	hard lemonade	375 mL
½ cup	liquid honey	125 mL
¼ cup	cold butter, cut in chunks	60 mL

• Remove the giblets and any excess fat from the chicken. Rinse and pat dry with paper towels. Place the chicken in the plastic bag.

• In a bowl, combine the orange juice concentrate, soy sauce, lime juice, cilantro, sesame oil, garlic, Jerk Seasoning and Rub, and pepper and whisk to blend well. Pour into the bag over the chicken and seal the bag, squeezing out excess air. Massage and turn the bag to distribute the marinade evenly over the chicken. Refrigerate for 4 to 6 hours or more.

GLAZE: In a small saucepan, bring the hard lemonade and honey to a boil and simmer for 3 or 4 minutes. Remove from heat and whisk in the butter, one chunk at a time, until it is all incorporated. Set aside.

• Preheat the grill to high (500°F/260°C).

• Remove the chicken from the bag and discard the marinade. Secure the chicken to the rotisserie rod according to the manufacturer's instructions, taking care to make sure it is balanced.

• Set the rotisserie on the grill, turn on the motor, place a foil pan directly under the chicken, and close the lid. Let the bird sear for 10 to 15 minutes.

• Turn the grill down to medium (350°F/175°C) and continue cooking for about 1 to 1½ hours, basting every 15 minutes with the glaze. Chicken is done when the juices run clear from the thigh or a meat thermometer inserted between the thigh and the body registers 165°F (74°C).

• Carefully remove the chicken from the rotisserie, being careful to avoid hot splatters. Cover the bird loosely with foil for 10 minutes to rest.

• Carve the chicken and set on a serving platter. Drizzle with more glaze and/or drippings.

Serves 4 to 6
Prep: 30 minutes
Marinade Time: 4 hours to overnight
Cook Time: 2 hours

BACON-WRAPPED CHICKEN DRUMSTICKS

Napoleon® Multi Basket

¼ cup	Garlic and Herb Rub (see recipe, page 26)	60 mL
1	chipotle pepper in adobo sauce, minced	1
1	Scotch bonnet chile, seeded and minced	1
1 tsp	sambal oelek (or other Asian chile sauce)	5 mL
12	chicken drumsticks, scored right through skin into meat in 3 or 4 places	12
12	slices bacon	12
4	cloves garlic, minced	4
½ cup	firmly packed brown sugar	125 mL
¼ cup	corn syrup	60 mL
2 tbsp	white wine vinegar	30 mL
1 tbsp	fresh herbs, chopped (parsley, sage, rosemary, etc.)	15 mL
¼ cup	Dijon mustard	60 mL
2 tbsp	grainy mustard	30 mL
	Salt and freshly ground black pepper	

• Mix together the Garlic and Herb Rub, chipotle, Scotch bonnet, and sambal oelek. Lightly score the drumsticks in several places all the way around. Rub the herb and hot pepper paste liberally into the drumsticks, pushing it into the scored meat. Note: Be very careful handling these hot peppers. If you have gloves, wear them. If not, take care to keep your hands away from sensitive areas like eyes and other places!

• Cover the rubbed chicken legs and refrigerate 4 hours or overnight.

• When ready to cook, wrap each drumstick with a slice of bacon and secure with a toothpick.

• In a bowl, whisk together the garlic, brown sugar, corn syrup, vinegar, herbs, and Dijon and grainy mustards. Season with salt and pepper. Set about ⅓ of sauce aside. Use the other ⅔ for basting.

• Preheat the grill to medium (350ºF/175ºC).

• Place the bacon-wrapped drumsticks in the basket.

• Grill the drumsticks, basting liberally with the sauce, until chicken is fully cooked and bacon is crisp, about 10 to 12 minutes a side. If you find the bacon is flaring up, turn one burner off and grill over indirect heat, closing the lid between bastes.

• When done, remove drumsticks from basket and place in a bowl. Pour the reserved sauce over and toss. Serve immediately or refrigerate to serve cold. Goes great with coleslaw, bread, and a few cold beverages.

Serve 6
Prep: 45 minutes
Marinade Time: 4 hours to overnight
Cook Time: 30 minutes

GRILLED CHICKEN BREASTS WITH MUSHROOM AND PEPPER STUFFED SKIN

Ask your butcher for at least 8-oz (250 g) breasts for this dish.

Napoleon® Multi Basket

¼ cup	cremini mushrooms, grilled and roughly chopped	60 mL
¼ cup	red bell peppers, finely diced	60 mL
¼ cup	Garlic and Herb Rub (see recipe, page 26)	60 mL
4	shallots, roughly chopped	4
1 tbsp	fresh sage, chopped	15 mL
2 tbsp	butter, melted	30 mL
¼ cup	fresh bread crumbs	60 mL
	Salt and freshly ground black pepper	
6	large skin-on chicken supremes (boneless breasts with the drumette still attached)	6

VINAIGRETTE

2 tbsp	cremini mushrooms, grilled and finely chopped	30 mL
¼ cup	Garlic and Herb Rub (see recipe, page 26)	60 mL
2 tsp	fresh sage, chopped	10 mL
¼ cup	frozen orange juice concentrate, thawed	60 mL
2 tbsp	red wine vinegar	30 mL
½ cup	extra-virgin olive oil	125 mL
	Salt and freshly ground pepper	
¼ cup	olive oil	60 mL

• Combine the ¼ cup (60 mL) mushrooms, red peppers, ¼ cup (60 mL) Garlic and Herb rub, shallots, 1 tbsp (15mL) sage, melted butter, and bread crumbs. Season with salt and pepper to taste.

• Set a chicken breast on a flat surface. With your fingers, gently push a pocket under the skin from beside the wing bone up over the top of the breast. Do not remove the skin entirely. Take 1 or 2 tbsp (15 to 30 mL) of the mushroom mixture and gently push it into the little pocket. Don't force too much in. The pocket should hold at least 1 to 2 tbsp, depending on the breast size. Secure the pocket with a toothpick and press down lightly to adhere seasoning mixture and skin to the breast. Cover the stuffed breasts and refrigerate for 1 hour. **Note:** This step is delicate but can be done, so don't rush. If the skin comes too loose, an extra toothpick and the basket will hold it in place.

VINAIGRETTE: In a saucepan, heat the 2 tbsp (30 mL) mushrooms, ¼ cup (60 mL) Garlic and Herb Rub, and 2 tsp (10 mL) sage over medium-high heat, stirring frequently. When thoroughly heated, add the orange juice, vinegar, and the oil and remove from the heat. Season with salt and pepper to taste. Set aside at room temperature.

• Preheat the grill to medium (350ºF/175ºC).

• Brush the inside of the basket with oil. Secure chicken breasts in the basket. Grill, skin side down first, brushing with the vinaigrette, about 8 to 10 minutes a side, or until a meat thermometer inserted into the thickest part of the breast registers 160ºF (71ºC).

• When done, remove the breasts very carefully from the basket, keeping the skin and stuffing intact. Serve the breasts with the vinaigrette, either whole or sliced and fanned on the plate.

Serves 6
Prep: 1 hour
Cook Time: 20 minutes

PLANKED RED WINE CHICKEN BREASTS
WITH A MUSHROOM AND BACON SAUCE

1–2	Napoleon® cedar planks, soaked overnight	
6	large skin-on chicken supremes (boneless breasts with the drumette still attached)	6
1	bunch fresh sage	1
3 cups	dry red wine, such as Pinot Noir or Shiraz	750 mL
2 tbsp	butter	30 mL
3	Vidalia or other sweet onions, cut in ¾-inch (2 cm) dice	3
1 lb	thick-sliced double-smoked bacon, cut in ¾-inch (2 cm) dice	500 g
4 cups	button and/or cremini mushrooms, quartered	1 L
4 cups	beef stock	1 L
	Salt and freshly ground black pepper	

• Place a chicken breast on a flat surface and use your fingers to gently push 4 or 5 sage leaves under the skin. Then press down on the skin to re-adhere to the flesh again.

• Place the breasts in a nonreactive dish and pour the wine over. Cover and refrigerate for 24 hours.

• Reserving the red wine, remove the chicken from the marinade and refrigerate until needed.

• In a saucepan, melt the butter over medium-high heat. Add the onions and bacon and sauté for 6 or 7 minutes. Add the mushrooms and sauté for another 10 minutes, stirring frequently, until browning and tender. Add the reserved wine and the beef stock and bring to a boil. Reduce slightly and simmer for about 30 minutes or until reduced by half Set aside, keeping warm, or reheat when chicken is ready. Season with salt and pepper to taste before serving.

• Preheat the grill to medium (350°F/175°C).

• Evenly space chicken supremes on the plank, place on the grill, and close lid. Plank-roast for 20 to 25 minutes or until chicken is golden and crisp. Chicken is done when juices run clear or a thermometer registers 160°F (71°C) when inserted into the thickest part of the breast.

• Serve the chicken breasts with a generous portion of the rich sauce.

Serves 6
Prep: 30 minutes
Marinade Time: 24 hours
Cook Time: 35 minutes

TIP: Have 1 or 2 large flat glass dishes, such as lasagna pans, on hand in your barbecue arsenal. They come in very handy for marinating chops and chicken breasts, etc.

GRILLED CITRUS CHICKEN BREASTS

6	boneless skinless chicken breasts (6 oz/175 g each)	6
2 tbsp	Tandoori Seasoning and Rub (see recipe, page 21)	30 mL
	Grated zest and juice of 1 lemon	
	Grated zest and juice of 1 orange	
	Grated zest and juice of 2 limes	
3	cloves garlic, minced	3
1	jalapeño pepper, finely chopped	1
1 tbsp	peeled and finely chopped fresh ginger	15 mL
1 tbsp	chopped fresh cilantro	15 mL
	Salt to taste	
2 cups	Papaya Salsa (see recipe, page 148)	

• Rub the chicken with the Tandoori Seasoning and Rub, massaging well into the meat.

• In a glass or other nonreactive dish, whisk together the lemon zest and juice, orange zest and juice, lime zest and juice, garlic, jalapeño, ginger, and cilantro.

• Add the chicken breasts to the marinade, turning to coat. Cover and refrigerate for 4 to 6 hours, but be careful not to leave chicken in this marinade for too long, as the citrus will begin to alter the texture of the chicken.

• Preheat the grill to medium-high (450°F/230°C).

• Remove chicken from the marinade, discarding the marinade, and season with salt. Grill for 5 to 6 minutes a side, or until golden brown and fully cooked (internal temperature of 160°F/71°C).

• Serve with a spoonful of Papaya Salsa on top.

Serves 6
Prep: 45 minutes
Marinade Time: 4 to 6 hours
Cook Time: 15 minutes

THANKSGIVING APPLE-SMOKED TURKEY
WITH CRABAPPLE GLAZE

Butcher's twine
2 bags Napoleon® Smoker Chips (hickory),
    soaked overnight
Napoleon® Smoker Tube
Napoleon® Poultry Stand (optional)

TURKEY RUB

¼ cup	granulated sugar	60 mL
2 tbsp	firmly packed light brown sugar	30 mL
2 tbsp	Rib and Chicken BBQ Seasoning and Rub (see recipe, page 17)	30 mL
1 tbsp	onion salt	15 mL
1 tbsp	celery salt	15 mL
2 tbsp	sweet paprika	30 mL
1 tbsp	rubbed dry sage	15 mL
1 tsp	freshly ground black pepper	5 mL
1	young turkey (12 to 14 lb/5.5 to 6 kg), preferably fresh	1
½ cup	olive oil	125 mL
2	Granny Smith apples, quartered and cored	2
2	medium onions, quartered	2
6	cloves garlic, lightly crushed	6
1 cup	apple juice	250 mL

GLAZE

2 cups	crabapple jelly	500 mL
½ cup	white wine, such as Riesling	125 mL
½ cup	pineapple juice	125 mL
½ cup	corn syrup	125 mL
2 tbsp	freshly squeezed lemon juice	30 mL
½ cup	South Carolina Yellow Mustard Barbecue Sauce (see recipe, page 43)	125 mL

Serves 6 to 8
Prep: 45 minutes
Cook Time: 3½ to 4 hours

Can be done on the rotisserie or a stand.

RUB: Combine the granulated sugar, brown sugar, Rib and Chicken BBQ Seasoning and Rub, onion salt, celery salt, paprika, sage, and pepper, and mix well.

• Remove the giblets and neck from turkey and rinse bird. Pat dry with paper towels.

• Rub the inside of the turkey with half of the olive oil and season thoroughly with half of the rub. Rub the rest of the oil on the outside of the turkey and massage in the rest of the seasoning, remembering to rub some right under the skin into the meat. Place the apples, onions, and garlic cloves in the cavity.

• Fold or tie the turkey wings back behind the bird and place the turkey, cavity down, over the Napoleon® Poultry Stand so that the stand protrudes far enough into the cavity to stand the bird upright and hold it firmly in place. Use the apple-onion mixture in the cavity to help stabilize the stand. (This is slightly awkward but well worth the effort.) Take care so the bird won't fall over once it's in the grill.

• Preheat the grill to medium (350º/175ºC), using the rear burner.

• Place the apple juice and some water in a drip pan deep enough to collect all the drippings from the turkey and place the whole bird over the pan. Place the smoker tube at the back of the grill, against the rear burner (If you choose to replenish the chips during the cooking time, be very careful) and close the lid. Baste from the dripping pan every 30 minutes.

GLAZE: In a saucepan, heat the crabapple jelly, wine, pineapple juice, corn syrup, and lemon juice just to a boil. Turn down the heat and simmer for 5 minutes. Stir in the South Carolina Yellow Mustard Barbecue Sauce and remove from the heat. Set aside until needed.

• Expect a 12-lb (5.5 kg) turkey to take between 3 and 3½ hours to reach 165ºF (74ºC) between the thigh and the breast. Be careful when checking not to contact bone with the thermometer.

• Baste the turkey every 15 minutes with the glaze for the last hour of the cooking time.

• When the turkey is done, use great care, gloves, and tongs when removing it from the grill. It should be allowed to rest, covered, for 20 minutes before carving.

• There will be some delicious juices in the drip pan. Use this liquid to make gravy if you wish.

TIP: Turkey off the grill is fabulous. But the most common error is overcooking. Every grill has its own personality. After about 2 hours and 45 minutes start checking the internal temp when you baste. A bird can cook a lot faster than you expect. If you overcook the bird it will be very dry and disappointing.

GRILLED CROSSBOW MANGO QUAIL

Twenty-four 7-inch (18 cm) metal or bamboo skewers (if using bamboo, soak them in water for at least 4 hours)

12	quails, butterflied	12
¼ cup	Rib and Chicken BBQ Seasoning and Rub (see recipe, page 17)	60 mL
¼ cup	olive oil	60 mL

MANGO SAUCE

¼ cup	dry white wine	60 mL
¼ cup	pure maple syrup	60 mL
¾ cup	Mango Barbecue Sauce (see recipe, page 50)	175 mL
1 tbsp	freshly cracked black pepper	15 mL
1 tbsp	chopped fresh lemon thyme	15 mL
2 tbsp	cold unsalted butter, cut in small chunks	30 mL
¾ cup	Mango Barbecue Sauce (see recipe, page 50)	175 mL
¼ cup	Southern Comfort liqueur	60 mL
1	slightly underripe mango, peeled, pitted, and sliced (optional)	1

Ask your butcher to butterfly and remove the backbone and rib cage of the quail.

• Rub the quail with the Chicken and Rib BBQ Seasoning and Rub, pressing some of the seasoning under the skin and into the flesh.

• To skewer, lay butterflied quails, meat side down, on a flat surface. Bring the legs up snug to the body of the quail. Skewer in an X pattern by inserting skewers into the thighs, under the leg bones, across through the opposite breasts, and exiting where the wings joins the bird. When done, the two skewers should form an X that holds the bird flat

• Brush each quail with a little olive oil and set aside.

MANGO SAUCE: In a small saucepan, whisk together the white wine, maple syrup, the ¾ cup (175 mL) Mango Barbecue Sauce, pepper, and thyme. Bring mixture to a low boil over medium-high heat, stirring constantly. Remove from heat and whisk in the cold butter, a few chunks at a time, until all the butter is incorporated. Set aside and keep warm.

• In a small saucepan, stir together the Mango Barbecue Sauce and Southern Comfort. Bring to a boil, reduce heat, and simmer for 4 to 5 minutes to reduce slightly and thicken. Set aside.

• Preheat grill to medium-high (450ºF/230ºC).

• Grill quails, skin side down, for 5 to 6 minutes. Turn and continue to cook for another 5 to 6 minutes, basting with the Southern Comfort mixture. Quail are done when juices run clear from a thigh pierced with a skewer.

• If using the mango, brush the slices with olive oil and grill 2 minutes a side to char slightly and heat through.

• Serve quail with the Maple Mango Sauce and grilled mango on the side.

Serves 6
Prep: 45 minutes
Cook Time: 15 minutes

GRILLED ASIAN CRISPY ORANGE DUCK BREASTS ON A PLANK

Untreated Napoleon® cedar plank, soaked overnight

¼ cup	frozen orange juice concentrate, thawed	60 mL
¼ cup	hoisin sauce	60 mL
1 tbsp	cider vinegar	15 mL
1 tbsp	fresh ginger, peeled and grated	15 mL
2 tsp	toasted sesame oil	10 mL
2	cloves garlic, minced	2
1	jalapeño pepper, seeded and diced finely	1
	Salt and freshly ground black pepper	
6	boneless skin-on Muscovy duck breasts (about 7 oz/200 g each)	6
1–2	navel oranges, sliced ¼ inch (0.5 cm) thick	1–2

• In a bowl, combine the orange juice concentrate, hoisin sauce, vinegar, ginger, sesame oil, garlic, jalapeño pepper, and salt and black pepper to taste.

• Trim the duck breasts of any skin or fat overlapping the edges. With a sharp knife, slash the skin several times without going into the flesh. Place the breasts in a resealable bag and pour the marinade over. Squeeze out the excess air and seal the bag, turning and massaging to coat the duck on all sides. Refrigerate for at least 2 to 4 hours.

• Preheat grill to medium-high (450ºF/230ºC).

• Remove breasts from marinade and place, skin side down, on the preheated grill. Grill for 3 to 4 minutes over direct heat.

• Lay the orange slices on the soaked plank in an overlapping blanket. Set the seared breasts on the orange slices and place the plank on one side of the grill. Turn the burner under the plank off and close the lid.

• Plank-roast the duck breasts for about 10 to 12 minutes. Duck should be crisp on the skin side and cooked to an internal temperature of 145ºF (63ºC).

• Slice the breasts in thin slices, maintaining the shape of the breast as you slice. Carefully fan the breasts on individual plates to serve.

NOTE: Duck meat is dense and flavourful like beef. It is best cooked medium-rare to just medium. It becomes very dry and chewy when overcooked.

Serves 6
Prep: 30 minutes
Marinade Time: 4 hours
Cook Time: 118 minutes

BUTTERMILK TURKEY THIGHS

WITH ALABAMA BARBECUE SAUCE

	Foodsafe plastic bag	
2 cups	buttermilk	500 mL
2 tbsp	Dijon mustard	30 mL
2 tbsp	liquid honey	30 mL
2 tbsp	fresh rosemary, finely chopped	30 mL
2 tsp	kosher salt	10 mL
1 tbsp	Rib and Chicken BBQ Seasoning and Rub (see recipe, page X)	15 mL
1 tsp	rubbed dry sage	5 mL
	Freshly ground black pepper to taste	
3	turkey thighs (about 1lb/500 g each)	3
1 cup	Memphis Style Barbecue Sauce or your favourite	250 mL

• In a bowl, combine the buttermilk, mustard, honey, rosemary, salt, Rib and Chicken BBQ Seasoning and Rub, sage, and pepper.

• Rinse the thighs and trim any excess fat or skin. Place them in a resealable bag and pour the marinade over. Press the excess air out and seal the bag. Turn and massage the thighs to coat them with the marinade and refrigerate for 4 to 6 hours or overnight.

• Preheat the grill to medium-high (450ºF/230ºC).

• Remove the thighs from the marinade and discard the marinade.

• Turn off one side of the grill. Place the thighs on the cool side and close the lid.

• Turn thighs after about 30 minutes and brush with Memphis-Style Barbecue Sauce. Brush several times until the juices run clear and the internal temperature registers 165ºF (74ºC), about 1 to 1½ hours.

• Remove thighs from the grill and wrap loosely in foil to rest for 10 minutes before carving and serving.

Serves 6 to 8
Prep: 30 minutes
Marinade Time: 4 hours to overnight
Cook Time: 1¾ hours

FISH AND SEAFOOD

CEDAR-PLANKED SALMON
TOPPED WITH TIGER SHRIMP

1 or 2 untreated Napoleon® cedar planks, soaked for 4 hours or overnight

TOPPING

1 tbsp	butter	15 mL
1	small red onion, chopped	1
3 tbsp	butter, melted	45 mL
2 tbsp	fresh chives, chopped	30 mL
2 tbsp	fresh dill, chopped	30 mL
2 tsp	grated lemon zest	10 mL
1 tbsp	freshly squeezed lemon juice	15 mL
½ cup	tiger shrimp (21–25 per lb/10–12 per kg), finely diced	125 mL
1 cup	panko (Japanese bread crumbs), lightly toasted	250 mL
1 tsp	salt	5 mL
1 tsp	freshly ground black pepper	5 mL
6	boneless skinless Atlantic salmon fillets (5–7 oz/150–200 g each)	6
2 tbsp	Seafood Seasoning and Rub (see recipe, page 22)	30 mL
12–18	whole tiger shrimp (21–25 per lb/10–12 per kg), peeled and deveined, tail on	12–18
	Olive oil or additional melted butter	
1 tbsp	Seafood Seasoning and Rub (see recipe, page 22)	15 mL
1	lemon, halved	1

TOPPING: In a skillet, heat the 1 tbsp (15 mL) butter over medium-high heat. Sauté the red onions for 4 to 5 minutes, stirring frequently, to soften and cook without browning. Stir in the melted butter, chives, dill, lemon zest and juice, and chopped shrimp and remove from the heat immediately. The shrimp should not be cooked at this point. Add the panko crumbs, salt, and pepper, and mix well.

• Evenly space the salmon fillets on the soaked plank(s). Divide the topping among the salmon fillets, gently packing and pressing to make it adhere. Split the whole tiger shrimp lengthwise down the middle about halfway to the tail. Set 2 or 3 shrimp on the topping, depending on the size of the fillet. Fan the shrimp out and overlap slightly. Lightly brush with the oil or butter and sprinkle with the Seafood Seasoning and Rub.

• Preheat grill to high (500°F/260°C).

• Carefully place the plank(s) on the grill and close the lid. Check occasionally if you hear it begin to crackle. If the plank is burning, use a spray bottle of water to douse the flames and move the plank to a cooler part of the grill.

• Plank-grill until salmon and shrimp are just cooked through, about 12 to 15 minutes. The shrimp should be just opaque and pink and the crust should be browning. Do not overcook, but be sure it's cooked through (a thermometer into the centre should read about 150°F/66°C).

• Squeeze a little lemon juice over the finished fillets and serve, smoking, on plank.

Serves 6
Prep Time: 1 hour
Cook Time: 15 minutes

PLANKED CRAB CAKES
WITH THAI CUCUMBER RELISH

1 or 2 untreated Napoleon® cedar planks, soaked for 4 hours or overnight

2 lbs	lump crabmeat, picked over for shells	1 kg
2	large eggs	2
½ cup	crushed soda crackers	125 mL
3 tbsp	Dijon mustard	45 mL
½ cup	mayonnaise (real, not whipped salad dressing)	125 mL
2 tsp	Worcestershire sauce	10 mL
2 tsp	Seafood Seasoning and Rub (see recipe, page 22) or Old Bay Seasoning	10 mL
	Salt and freshly ground black pepper	

THAI CUCUMBER RELISH

1⅓ cups	coconut vinegar or rice vinegar	325 mL
1½ cups	water	375 mL
1⅓ cups	granulated sugar	325 mL
1	2-inch piece of fresh ginger, peeled and julienned	1
2	shallots, thinly sliced	2
1 cup	English cucumber, finely diced	250 mL
1 tbsp	coarsely chopped fresh cilantro	15 mL
2	Thai birdseye chiles, cut in very thin strips	2

• Combine the crabmeat with the eggs, crackers, mustard, mayonnaise, Worcestershire sauce, Seafood Seasoning and Rub, and salt and pepper. Mix very well.

• Form the crab mixture into cakes about 3 or 4 inches (7.5 to 10 cm) in diameter and 1 inch (2.5 cm) thick. As is true for burger patties, the more uniform in size and thickness, the better.

• Evenly space the crab cakes on the plank(s). Cover with plastic wrap and refrigerate for 1 hour to rest.

THAI CUCUMBER RELISH: In a saucepan, boil the vinegar, water, and sugar for 5 minutes. Remove from the heat and add the ginger, shallots, and cucumber. Stir and set aside to cool. Stir in the cilantro and pepper when cool. Set aside at room temperature.

• Preheat the grill to medium-high (450°F/230°C).

• Set the planked crab cakes on the grill, close the lid, and plank-bake for 12 to 15 minutes, or until cooked through.

• Remove crab cakes from plank and serve 2 to 3 per person, topped with cucumber relish.

Serves 6 to 8
Prep Time: 1 hour
Resting Time: 1 hour
Cook Time: 15 minutes

GRILLED TUNA STEAK NIÇOISE

2 tbsp	extra-virgin olive oil	30 mL
2 tbsp	Grill-Roasted Garlic (see recipe, page 56), mashed	30 mL
2 tbsp	freshly squeezed lemon juice	30 mL
6	tuna steaks (6–8 oz/175–250 g each), 1 inch (2.5 cm) thick	6
	Coarse sea salt	
5	whole anchovies, drained and coarsely chopped	5
¼ cup	fresh lemon juice	60 mL
1 tbsp	Grill-Roasted Garlic (see recipe, page 56)	15 mL
¼ cup	freshly grated Parmesan cheese	60 mL
¼ cup	grainy Dijon mustard	60 mL
½ cup	extra-virgin olive oil	125 mL
	Coarse sea salt and freshly ground pepper	
6	just ripe (not overripe) grape tomatoes, halved	6
1 lb	tiny new potatoes, red or white, cooked until just tender and halved	500 g
½ lb	green beans, steamed until just tender	250 g
1	bunch radishes, trimmed and quartered	1
1	large yellow bell pepper, seeded and cut in 1-inch (2.5 cm) pieces	1
½ cup	pitted black olives	125 mL
6	hard-cooked eggs, quartered	6
	Lemon wedges	
2 tbsp	fresh basil, chopped	30 mL

• Whisk together the 2 tbsp (30 mL) oil, 2 tbsp (30 mL) Grill-Roasted Garlic, and 2 tbsp (30 mL) lemon juice. Place the tuna steaks in a nonreactive dish large enough to hold them in a single layer. Pour the garlic and oil mixture over them and massage it in to coat each steak thoroughly. Season with sea salt to taste and cover. Refrigerate for 30 minutes.

• Place the anchovies, ¼ cup (60 mL) lemon juice, 1 tbsp (15 mL) Grill-Roasted Garlic, Parmesan, and mustard in a food processor. Process briefly to mix. With the processor on, slowly drizzle in the ½ cup (125 mL) olive oil.

• Place the tomatoes, potatoes, green beans, radishes, bell pepper, and olives in a bowl. Pour half the dressing over and gently toss the vegetables to coat.

• Preheat the grill to medium-high (450°F/230°C).

• Grill the tuna steaks 3 to 4 minutes a side for medium, or until the fish just yields when pushed on with a finger. Do not overcook tuna.

• Place the salad mixture on a platter or individual plates. Place the tuna over the salad and drizzle the rest of the dressing on. Garnish the platter or plates with the egg and lemon wedges and sprinkle with basil. Serve immediately with fresh baguette on the side.

Serves 6
Prep Time: 1 hour
Marinating Time: 30 minutes
Cook Time: 10 minutes

GRILLED HALIBUT STEAK
WITH BAY SCALLOPS AND HERB BUTTER SAUCE

Napoleon® Grill Topper

3 tbsp	olive oil	45 mL
3 tbsp	Grill-Roasted Garlic (see page 56)	45 mL
	Sea salt	
3	halibut fillets (about 12 oz/375 g each), 1½ to 2 inches (4 to 5 cm) thick	3
2 tbsp	butter	30 mL
2 tsp	grated lime zest	10 mL
¼ cup	freshly squeezed lime juice	60 mL
1 tbsp	granulated sugar	15 mL
1–1½ lbs	fresh bay scallops in their liquor	500 to 750 g
1½ tbsp	fresh cilantro, chopped	22 mL
1½ tbsp	fresh basil, chopped	22 mL
1½ tbsp	fresh mint, chopped	22 mL
½ cup	cold butter, in pieces	125 mL
	Salt and freshly ground black pepper	
1	lime (or more), quartered	1

• Preheat the grill to medium-high (450º/230º).

• Mix the oil, Grill-Roasted Garlic, and sea salt together. Set the halibut steaks in the Napoleon® Grill Topper and rub the garlic mixture on both sides.

• Place the grill topper with the halibut on the grill and close the lid. Grill-roast the fish for 8 to 10 minutes a side or more, depending on thickness. Fish is done when it just yields to the touch. Don't overcook.

• Preheat a large skillet on the side burner of your grill. When you turn the halibut, put the 2 tbsp (30 mL) butter in the pan and add the lime juice to the melting butter. Stir in the lime zest and sugar. As soon as it bubbles, pour in the bay scallops with their liquor and the chopped herbs (they cook very quickly). As soon as the pan starts to bubble again, 1 or 2 minutes at most, remove from the burner and stir in the cold butter, one piece at a time. Season with salt and pepper to taste and set back on the warm burner (*but don't turn the heat back on*) while you remove the halibut from the grill.

• The halibut and the scallops and sauce should be done at about the same time. Cut the halibut steaks in half and place on individual warmed plates or a platter. Spoon the scallops and butter sauce generously over the fish, garnish with the lime quarters, and serve immediately.

Serves 6
Prep Time: 45 minutes
Cook Time: 15 minutes

GRILLED TEQUILA SUNRISE SWORDFISH STEAK
WITH SWORDFISH SEVICHE

2 cups	fish stock	500 mL
¾ cup	frozen orange juice concentrate, thawed	175 mL
⅔ cup	tequila	150 mL
1 tbsp	grated lime zest	15 mL
¼ cup	freshly squeezed lime juice	60 mL
6 tbsp	granulated sugar	90 mL
¼ cup	orange liqueur, such as Triple Sec	60 mL
2 tsp	ground coriander	10 mL
	Salt and freshly ground black pepper	
6	swordfish steaks (6–8 oz/175–250 g each), 1 inch (2.5 cm) thick	6

SEVICHE

2 cups	swordfish, cut in ¼- to ½-inch (0.5 to 1 cm) cubes	500 mL
1 cup	peeled seedless orange segments	250 mL
¾ cup	peeled seedless lime segments	175 mL
¼ cup	freshly squeezed lime juice	60 mL
2 tbsp	coarse sea salt	30 mL
2 tbsp	freshly cracked black pepper	30 mL
2 tbsp	olive oil	30 mL
2	oranges, sliced	2
2 tbsp	chopped fresh cilantro	30 mL
	Lime wedges	

• In a nonreactive bowl, whisk together the fish stock, orange juice concentrate, tequila, 1 tbsp (15 mL) lime zest, ¼ cup (60 mL) lime juice, sugar, orange liqueur, coriander, and salt and pepper to taste. Place half the mixture in a glass bowl and half the mixture in a dish large enough to hold the swordfish steaks in one layer.

• Place the steaks in the marinade and turn back and forth to coat both sides. Cover and refrigerate for 30 minutes only. Do not leave too long in the marinade, as the citrus will cook the fish.

SEVICHE: Add the cubed swordfish, orange segments, lime segments, and lime juice to the other half in the bowl. Cover and refrigerate for 1 hour (or up to overnight).

• Preheat grill to medium-high (450ºF/230ºC).

• Remove the swordfish steaks from the marinade and sprinkle both sides with the 2 tbsp (30 mL) coarse salt and 2 tbsp (30 mL) cracked pepper. Brush the grill with the olive oil and grill the steaks until just cooked through, or until the fish flakes easily, about 4 to 5 minutes a side.

• Serve the steaks with the seviche spooned over them. Top with orange slices and sprinkle with cilantro. Garnish with lime wedges on the side.

Serves 6
Prep Time: 1 hour
Marinating Time: 1 hour
Cook Time: 10 minutes

GRILLED WHISKEY SALMON FILLETS

1 cup	whiskey, a good scotch or your favourite	250 mL
⅔ cup	light soy sauce	150 mL
4	cloves garlic, puréed	4
¼ cup	olive oil	60 mL
6	boneless salmon fillets (6–8 oz/175–250 g each)	6
2 tbsp	Asian chile paste	30 mL
⅔ cup	whiskey	150 mL
5	green onions, thinly sliced on the diagonal	5
10–12	thin slices fresh ginger	10–12
2 tsp	blended sesame oil	10 mL
2 tbsp	liquid honey	30 mL
¼ cup	water	60 mL
¼ cup	olive oil	60 mL

• Whisk the 1 cup (250 mL) whiskey, soy sauce, garlic, and olive oil in a dish large enough to hold the salmon fillets in a single layer.

• Place the fillets in the marinade and turn skin side up. Cover and refrigerate for 4 to 6 hours. Do not leave any more than 8 hours or texture of the fish will begin to be affected.

• In a saucepan, combine the chile paste, ⅔ cup (150 mL) whiskey, green onions, ginger, sesame oil, honey, and water. Bring just to the boil and simmer, uncovered, until reduced by half and thickened to a syrup. Keep sauce warm while you grill the salmon.

• Preheat the grill to medium-high (450ºF/230ºC).

• Remove the salmon from the marinade, reserving marinade to baste. Brush the grate with the ¼ cup (60 mL) olive oil, and place the salmon on the preheated grill, skin side up. Grill for 5 to 7 minutes a side, or until just cooked, basting with the marinade. Discard any marinade left when salmon is done.

• Remove salmon fillets from grill and serve with the warm sauce drizzled over top.

TIP: It is important to preheat the grill for fish. If you set the fish on a good hot grill you will be able to turn the fish easily when it is ready. If it does not yield, leave it for a minute or two and try again. Don't destroy it trying to force a turn. It will yield easily *when it is ready*. When you are ready to remove it from the grill if you have done the job right you will be able to slide the spatula between the skin and the meat and lift the fillet away from the skin.

Serves 6
Prep Time: 45 minutes
Marinating Time: 4 to 6 hours
Cook Time: 15 minutes

BASKET-GRILLED WHOLE RAINBOW TROUT
STUFFED WITH APPLE AND LEMONGRASS

Napoleon® Fish Basket

4	stalks lemongrass (light green, not old)	4
½ cup	fresh herbs (such as chervil, parsley, tarragon), chopped	125 mL
1 tbsp	lime zest	5 mL
1 tbsp	freshly squeezed lime juice	15 mL
3	apples (such as Gala or Granny Smith), peeled and grated	3
1	small red onion, peeled, trimmed, and sliced thinly	1
¾ cup	butter, melted	175 mL
1 cup	panko (Japanese bread crumbs)	250 mL
2 tsp	kosher salt	10 mL
2 tsp	freshly cracked black pepper	10 mL
2	whole rainbow trout (2–3 lbs/1–1.5 kg) cleaned, head on or off as preferred	2
½ cup	butter, melted	125 mL
	Lemon wedges	

• Peel 1 or 2 of the heaviest outer layers off the lemongrass stocks and cut off the darkest green ends and discard. Finely mince the tender white and lightest green parts.

• Combine the lemongrass, herbs, lime zest and juice, apples, onion, ¾ cup (175 mL) butter, panko, salt, and pepper. Toss to mix well and to distribute the juice and butter.

• Push the stuffing lightly into the cavities in the fish. Don't pack them too tightly or the fish will burst.

• Preheat the grill to medium-high (450ºF/230ºC).

• Brush the outsides of the fish with some of the ½ cup (125 mL) of melted butter. Place them end to end in the Napoleon® Fish Basket and close the basket. They should be held firmly in place.

• Set the basket on the grill and roast the trout for 10 to 12 minutes a side, or until just cooked through. Trout is a delicate fish — do not overcook.

• Carefully remove the fish from the basket. Serve each guest a generous portion of the fish, drizzled with a little melted butter, stuffing on the side and lots of lemon wedges. A bottle of ice-cold Riesling may also be called for.

Serves 4 to 6
Prep Time: 1 hour
Cook Time: 25 minutes

GRILLED JUMBO SAMBUCA SHRIMP
WITH SPICY TOMATO CREAM

Napoleon® Meat Injector

½ cup	sambuca liqueur	125 mL
12-16	very large tiger shrimp (2–4 per lb/4–6 per kg), peeled and deveined, tail on	12-16
¼ cup	freshly squeezed lime juice	60 mL
1 tbsp	puréed garlic	15 mL
1 tbsp	puréed fresh ginger	15 mL
½ tsp	turmeric	2 mL

SPICY TOMATO CREAM

2 tbsp	coconut oil or vegetable oil	30 mL
1 tsp	yellow mustard seeds	5 mL
½ tsp	fenugreek seeds	2 mL
2 tsp	curry powder	10 mL
2 tsp	chili powder	10 mL
1 tsp	turmeric	5 mL
1–2	Scotch bonnet chiles, minced	1–2
3	cloves garlic, minced	3
2 tsp	fresh ginger, peeled and grated	10 mL
3	medium onions, diced	3
1 cup	crushed tomatoes	250 mL
2 tsp	tamarind paste	10 mL
½ cup	water	125 mL
¼ cup	whipping (35%) cream	60 mL

• Pull the sambuca into the injector. Insert the needle once or twice and inject about 1 tbsp (15 mL) of the liqueur into each shrimp. Place the shrimp in a flat dish.

• Whisk together the lime juice, puréed garlic, puréed ginger, and turmeric.

• Pour over the shrimp and toss to coat. Cover and refrigerate for 1 hour.

SPICY TOMATO CREAM: In a large saucepan, heat the coconut oil over medium heat. Stir in the mustard seeds, fenugreek seeds, curry powder, chili powder, and turmeric and stir in the oil for 1 minute. Add the chiles, minced garlic, and grated ginger and continue stirring for 1 minute more. Add the onion and sauté, stirring frequently, until the onions are golden. Do not try to rush this or the onions and spices will burn. If the mixture is browning too quickly, lower the temperature in the pan by adding 1 tbsp (15 mL) of cold water, which will cook off as it cools the pan. This step should take about 10 or 15 minutes.

• Add the tomatoes, tamarind, and water and bring to a boil. Turn off the heat, add the cream, and mix well. Keep warm.

• Preheat the grill to medium (350ºF/175ºC).

• Remove the shrimp from the marinade, discard marinade, and grill shrimp until just cooked through, about 4 to 5 minutes a side, or until opaque, pink, and just firm to the touch. Do not overcook these shrimp.

• Serve 2 shrimp to a serving, with warm sauce on the side.

Serves 6
Prep Time: 1 hour
Marinating Time: 1 hour
Cook Time: 15 minutes

GRILL TOPPER PICKEREL
WITH A SHRIMP AND SPINACH CRUST

Napoleon® Grill Topper

1 tbsp	olive oil	15 mL
1	small onion, finely diced	1
3	cloves garlic, minced	3
2	red chiles, minced	2
2 tbsp	white wine	30 mL
1 tbsp	freshly squeezed lemon juice	15 mL
3 tbsp	very thinly sliced fresh sorrel leaves	45 mL
	or	
1½ tbsp	chopped fresh tarragon	22 mL
3 cups	baby spinach leaves, stems removed and thoroughly washed	750 mL
1 cup	cold-water baby shrimp, thawed if frozen, and drained	250 mL
½ cup	cream cheese, softened	125 mL
4 tbsp	Seafood Seasoning and Rub (see recipe, page 22) or Old Bay Seasoning	60 mL
⅔ cup	panko (Japanese bread crumbs), or more	150 mL
	Salt and freshly ground black pepper	
2 tbsp	olive oil	30 mL
6–8	pickerel fillets (6 oz/175 g each)	6–8

• In a large skillet, heat the oil over medium-high heat and sauté the onion for 3 to 4 minutes. Add the garlic and continue cooking for 2 minutes without letting the garlic brown. Add the chiles and continue to sauté for 2 or 3 minutes, until mixture is soft and fragrant. Add the white wine, lemon juice, sorrel, (or tarragon) and spinach all at once and cook, stirring, until the spinach has begun to wilt but has not lost its brightness and most of the moisture has evaporated, about 2 minutes at most. Cool for 15 minutes.

• Add the shrimp, cream cheese, and Seafood Seasoning and Rub. Mix to blend the ingredients evenly. Stir in the panko crumbs and adjust seasoning with salt and pepper. This mixture can be frozen, well wrapped, for up to 1 month.

• Preheat the grill to medium-high (450°F/230°C).

• Drizzle a little olive oil on the Napoleon® Grill Topper and set the pickerel fillets on it. Spread some of the shrimp topping over each fillet, evenly covering the whole surface of the fillet with a layer about ½ to ¾ inch (1 to 2 cm) thick.

• Place the topper on the grill and close the lid. Grill-bake the fish for about 8 to 10 minutes, or until the topping is hot and golden brown and the fish is just cooked and flakes easily.

• Remove from the heat, place fillets on individual plates, and serve immediately.

Serves 6
Prep Time: 1 hour
Cook Time: 10 minutes

BARBECUED OYSTERS NAPOLEON

Napoleon® Grill Topper

1 tbsp	olive oil	15 mL
½	small onion, finely diced	½
2	cloves garlic, minced	2
4 cups	spinach, packed	1 L
2 tbsp	cognac	30 mL
6 tbsp	goat cheese	90 mL
¼ cup	coarse bread crumbs	60 mL
½ cup	crisp-cooked diced bacon (about 8 slices)	125 mL
	Salt and freshly ground black pepper	
12–18	fresh oysters, shucked	12–18
1	lemon	1
	Lemon wedges	

• In a large pan over high heat on the grill side burner, or on the stovetop, heat the oil and sauté the onion and garlic for 2 or 3 minutes, until fragrant and tender. Add the spinach and stir just until wilted, 1 to 2 minutes. Add the cognac all at once and carefully allow to flame. As soon as flame stops, remove from the heat and drain.

• Place the spinach mixture in a bowl and add the goat cheese, bread crumbs, and bacon. Season with salt and pepper.

• Centre a shucked oyster on its shell and set 1 tbsp (15 mL) of the spinach mixture on top. Repeat until all the oysters are topped.

• Preheat the grill to medium-high (450ºF/230ºC)

• Place the oysters on the Napoleon® Grill Topper and set on the grill. Close the lid and grill-bake for 3 to 5 minutes, until the cheese is browning and bubbly. Give each oyster a squeeze of lemon juice.

• Remove from the grill and serve immediately with lemon wedges and lots of crusty bread to mop up all the juices.

Serves 2 as a main course, 6 to 8 as an appetizer
Prep Time: 1 hour
Cook Time: 5 minutes

GRILLED LOBSTER THERMIDOR
WITH A CRAB AND BRIE CRUST

2	fresh live lobsters (1½–2 lb/1.5–1 kg each)	2
1½ cups	beer	375 mL
1 tbsp	Hot and Spicy BBQ Seasoning and Rub (see recipe, page 18)	15 mL
½ cup	butter	125 mL
½ cup	cream cheese, softened	125 mL
½ cup	ranch dressing	125 mL
¼ cup	whipping (35%) cream	60 mL
1	medium sweet onion, grilled and chopped	1
6	large white mushrooms, grilled and coarsely chopped	6
1	green onion, chopped	1
2	cloves garlic, minced	2
1 cup	crabmeat	250 mL
1 cup	Brie cheese, cut in ½-inch (1 cm) cubes	250 mL
2 tbsp	fresh thyme, chopped	30 mL
½ cup	crispy fried onions (available at Asian supermarkets)	125 mL
	Salt and freshly ground black pepper	
¼ cup	freshly grated Parmesan cheese	60 mL

• Lay lobsters on a clean flat surface and, with a large, very sharp knife, split them in half lengthwise. You should have two identical halves, each with half a tail, body, and head section. Remove the recognizable sac from the head sections and the long grey-black threads from each body. Then discard "granny's rocker," the bony bits and feathery gills from the head. Remove the elastic bands from the claws last. When you are looking at 4 dressed lobster halves, drizzle them with a little beer on the meat sides.

• Spray lobster meat with nonstick cooking spray and sprinkle with a little of the hot seasoning mix.

• Preheat the grill to medium-high (450ºF/230ºC).

• Set a small saucepan on the side burner and slowly heat the remaining beer and butter over low heat. Once butter is melted, whisk and set aside, keeping warm.

• In a bowl, mix together the cream cheese, ranch dressing, and cream. Stir in the grilled onions and mushrooms, green onion, garlic, crabmeat, Brie, thyme, and crispy fried onion. Season with salt and pepper to taste and set aside.

• Place lobsters on the preheated grill, meat side down, and grill for 1 to 2 minutes, until shell begins to turn colour. Turn lobsters, baste the meat with the beer butter, continuing to grill.

• At this point top each lobster half with one-quarter of the crab and Brie mixture and sprinkle with the Parmesan cheese. Reduce heat to medium-low (250ºF/120ºC) and close lid. Grill-bake for 6 to 8 minutes, until lobsters are fully cooked and the cheese is just melting and bubbling. Be careful not to overcook.

• Serve immediately.

Serves 4 to 6

TIP: Shellfish is often the victim of a lack of knowledge. Lobster, shrimp, crab, and scallops are so frequently overcooked in restaurants that few people have actually eaten them properly cooked. These take very little time to cook. In the case of scallops, it's seconds. The meat should have just turned opaque and pink. It should be barely firm to the touch and the texture should be dense but yielding — not chewy. The butter or sauce is there to enhance a delicate flavour not disguise a rubbery dry result.

Prep Time: 1 hour
Cook Time: 15 minutes

GRILLED CHOCOLATE LOBSTER TAILS

Napoleon® Grill Topper

6–8	lobster tails (6–8 oz/175–250 g each), thawed if frozen	6–8
1½ tbsp	Grill-Roasted Garlic (see recipe, page 56)	22 mL
1 tbsp	olive oil	15 mL
2 tbsp	bittersweet chocolate, grated	30 mL
1–2 tbsp	chipotle chiles in adobo sauce	15–30 mL
2 tsp	fresh cilantro, chopped	10 mL
1 tsp	freshly ground black pepper	5 mL
	Salt to taste	
⅔ cup	beer	150 mL
½ cup	butter, melted	125 mL
½ cup	grated bittersweet chocolate	125 mL
¼ cup	panko (Japanese bread crumbs)	60 mL
½ cup	pecans, peanuts, or cashews, crushed	125 mL
	Lemon slices	

• Lay lobster tails on a clean flat surface and, with a very sharp knife or good kitchen shears, cut through the top shell, end to end. You can go right into the meat, but you don't want to go all the way through the back shell. Once you've made this cut, take the tail in your hands and firmly break it open enough to work your fingers under the tail meat and free it from the shell. Then pull it up out of the shell while leaving it still attached at the end. Push the halves back together and lay the tail meat back down on the shell. You now have a lobster tail on a stand that should sit steady. This is not a pleasant job, but it's well worth the effort. Be patient. And be careful — some nasty wounds have resulted from a battle with lobster tails. You should end up with 6 to 8 lobster tails, each of which you will cut open, slightly more than halfway through the meat, length-wise, if you didn't already while freeing the tail.

• Place the lobster tails in a flat nonreactive dish and refrigerate if not using immediately. Unlike meat, shellfish must be used quickly and kept cold.

• In a bowl, combine the roasted garlic, oil, 2 tbsp (30 mL) chocolate, chipotle, cilantro, and black pepper and mix well. Pack some of this mixture into the split down each tail. Cover and refrigerate for 30 minutes to let the lobster marinate.

• In one bowl, combine the beer with the melted butter.

• In another bowl, combine the ½ cup (125 mL) chocolate, panko, and nuts and mix well.

• Preheat the grill to medium-high (450ºF/230ºC).

• Place the tails on the Napoleon® Grill Topper and place in the grill. Grill for 3 to 4 minutes with the lid down. Baste with the beer butter and close lid for another 2 to 3 minutes. Open lid and baste once more, then sprinkle with the chocolate-nut mixture. Close the lid for a final 2 to 3 minutes. Lobster should be just cooked through. Depending on the size of the tails, you may want more or less time.

• Serve immediately garnished with grilled lemon slices. (Just before serving place the lemon slices on the grill for about 45 seconds to char.)

Serves 6 to 8
Prep Time: 1 hour
Marinade Time: 30 minutes
Cook Time: 10 minutes

DESSERTS

PLANK-SMOKED CHOCOLATE BROWNIES WITH GOOEY MARSHMALLOW TOPPING

1 cup	butter	250 mL
8 oz	unsweetened chocolate, coarsely chopped	250 mL
5 large	eggs	
1 tbsp	vanilla	15 mL
3½ cups	sugar	875 mL
½ tsp	salt	2 mL
1¾ cups	all-purpose flour	435 mL
2 tsp	baking powder	10 mL
½ cup + 1 cup	semi sweet chocolate chips	125 mL +250 mL
½ cup + 1 cup	white chocolate, coarsely chopped	125 mL +250 mL
½ cup + 1 cup	macadamia nuts, coarsely chopped	125 mL +250 mL
½ cup	smooth peanut butter	125 mL
½ cup	raspberry jam	125 mL
2	untreated cedar plank, soaked at least 12 hours.	

• Generously grease a 9" X 13" pan. Sift together the flour and baking powder.

• Melt butter and chocolate over low heat in a heavy saucepan, stirring occasionally. When melted, remove from the heat and let cool slightly.

• In a large mixing bowl beat eggs, vanilla, sugar, and salt for 10 minutes at medium speed. Blend in the chocolate butter mixture at low speed until just mixed. Don't over beat.

• Fold gently into the chocolate egg mixture until just blended.

• Gently stir in 1 cup each of chocolate chips, white chocolate and macadamia nuts.

• Preheat the grill to medium or a touch higher (375°F/190°C).

• Pour the brownie mixture into the prepared pan and gently smooth to level. Spread the topping mixture over the brownie mix.

• Set the soaked plank on the grill. Set the brownies in the pan on the plank. Close the grill lid and bake for 40 to 45 minutes until an inserted toothpick comes out clean.

• Cool for several hours to overnight.

• Turn the brownie pan upside down and remove the brownies.

• Place the entire brownie slab on soaked plank. You may have to cut the slab a little to make it fit, leaving an edge of the plank around the brownie.

• Spread peanut butter over brownie in an even layer.

• Spread raspberry jam over peanut butter in an even layer.

• In a bowl combine mini marshmallows, chocolate chips, white chocolate chips and macadamia nuts.

• Scatter the marshmallow mixture over the brownies.

• Place on preheated medium-low grill and close lid.

• Plank warm the brownies until the marshmallows are golden brown, the topping gooey and the brownies are warm.

• Remove from grill and serve with ice cream.

Makes 18 to 24 squares
Prep Time: 30 minutes
Cook Time: 45 minutes

GRILLED PINEAPPLE, PEACH, AND BLUEBERRY CRUMBLE

1	baking dish large enough to hold 3 qts/ litres, buttered	
½ cup	melted butter	125 mL
1	fresh pineapple, peeled, cored, and sliced in 1-inch (2.5 cm) slices	1
3	medium peaches, peeled, pitted, and sliced in 1-inch (2/5 cm) wedges	3
1 cup	blueberries, washed and picked over	250 mL
2 tbsp	crystallized ginger, chopped	30 mL
¼ cup	dark rum, such as Appleton	60 mL
⅔ cup	unsweetened shredded coconut	150 mL
½ cup	firmly packed brown sugar	125 mL
¼ cup	all-purpose flour	60 mL
⅓ cup	sliced toasted almonds, roughly chopped	75 mL
½ cup	butter, melted	125 mL
	Whipped cream or ice cream	

- Preheat grill to medium (350ºF/175ºC).

- Brush the ½ cup (125 mL) melted butter over both sides of the peach and pineapple slices. Place the peach slices on the grill for 1 minute on each side. Cut into 1-inch (2.5 cm) chunks and place in prepared dish. Grill the pineapple slices for 5 to 6 minutes a side, until well marked. Cut into 1-inch (2.5 cm) chunks and add to the peaches. Add the blueberries, ginger, and rum and mix well.

- Combine the coconut, brown sugar, flour, almonds, and ½ cup (125 mL) melted butter. Mix very well. Sprinkle this mixture evenly over the pineapple mixture.

- Preheat grill to medium (350ºF/175ºC).

- Set baking dish on the grill and close the lid. Grill-bake for 25 to 30 minutes, or until the fruit is tender and the topping is golden and crunchy.

- Serve with whipped cream or ice cream on the side.

Serves 6 to 8
Prep Time: 30 minutes
Cook Time: 30 minutes

GRILLED PEACH AND RASPBERRY PARFAIT

6 parfait glasses

3	large firm but ripe peaches, peeled, pitted, and halved	3
3 tbsp	amaretto liqueur, divided, plus more for drizzling	45 mL
1 cup	whipping (35%) cream, chilled	250 mL
2 tsp	rum	10 mL
2 cups	crushed amaretti cookies	500 mL
2 cups	raspberries, fresh or frozen and thawed	500 mL
1	1-quart (1 L) container French vanilla ice cream	1
½ cup	sliced toasted almonds	125 mL

• Place the peach halves in a bowl and pour the amaretto over them. Toss to coat and let sit for 20 to 30 minutes.

• Preheat the grill to medium-high (450ºF/230ºC).

• Place the peaches, cut side down first, on the grill and leave for at least 2 minutes without touching. You want grill marks, and if they're moved too much, they won't mark. Once they are tender and marked, remove them from the grill and cut in ½-inch (1 cm) dice.

• Whip the cream with the rum until stiff peaks form.

• Place 3 or 4 pieces of peach in the bottom of each of 6 parfait glasses. Top with 4 or 5 raspberries and drizzle about 1 tsp (5 mL) amaretto over the fruit. Cover with 1 to 2 tbsp (15 to 30 mL) crushed amaretti and some ice cream. Repeat these steps one more time. Finish with fruit and amaretti and top with the whipped cream and a few slivered almonds.

Serves 6
Prep Time: 30 minutes
Marinate Time: 30 minutes
Cook Time: 5 minutes

ICE WINE PEARS IN FOIL

6 sheets of heavy-duty aluminum foil, each about 12 by 12 inches (30 by 30 cm)

6	Bosc pears, peeled	6
2 tbsp	dried currants	30 mL
1 tbsp	grated lemon zest	15 mL
1	375 mL bottle icewine, at room temperature	1
6 tbsp	liquid honey	90 mL
6	sprigs fresh mint	6
	ground nutmeg (fresh grated if you have it)	
1 tbsp	frozen orange juice concentrate, thawed	15 mL
6	scoops good-quality vanilla ice cream, such as Häagen Daz	6
	Mint sprigs	
	Fresh berries of choice (optional)	

• Place a pear in the centre of each square of aluminum foil. Draw the corners up slightly to form a bowl shape. Top each pear with 1 tsp (5 mL) currants and ½ tsp (2 mL) lemon peel. Drizzle with 1 tbsp (15 mL) icewine and 1 tbsp (15 mL) honey. Add a sprig of mint and a tiny pinch of nutmeg.

• Draw the corners of the foil up around each pear and crimp the edges to form a tightly sealed bundle.

• Preheat the grill to medium-high (450ºF/230ºC).

• Place bundles on one side of the grill and turn the burner under that side off so that they receive indirect heat. Close the lid. Grill-roast pouches for 30 to 45 minutes, or until the pears are tender.

• Meanwhile, place the rest of the bottle of icewine and the orange juice concentrate in a small saucepan on the side burner. Bring to a gentle boil and simmer to reduce slightly to a syrupy consistency. Set aside until the pears are ready.

• Remove the bundles to plates. Open carefully (watch out for steam!) and slide contents onto the plate. Garnish with a scoop of vanilla ice cream, drizzle with the icewine syrup, and place a fresh mint sprig on top. Serve immediately.

• For extra pizzazz, add just a few fresh berries, but don't overwhelm the scrumptious pear.

Serves 6
Prep Time: 30 minutes
Cook Time: 45 minutes

GRILLED CHOCOLATE BANANA BURRITOS

¾ cup	creamy peanut butter	175 mL
6	8-inch (20 cm) flour tortillas	6
3	ripe bananas, peeled	3
1½ cup	miniature marshmallows	375 mL
¾ cup	semisweet mini chocolate chips	175 mL
½ cup	butter, melted	125 mL
	Vanilla ice cream	
	Fresh strawberries	

• Preheat grill to medium (350ºF/175ºC).

• Spread 2 tbsp (30 mL) peanut butter on each tortilla.

• Grill bananas for 3 to 4 minutes, or until lightly charred and heated through. Remove from grill and split in half lengthwise. Lay a banana half on each of the peanut-buttered tortillas.

• Sprinkle ¼ cup (60 mL) marshmallows and 2 tbsp (30 mL) chocolate chips on each tortilla. Roll up the tortilla, folding in the ends as you go.

• Brush the burritos lightly with butter and place on the preheated grill. Cook for 3 to 4 minutes a side, or until heated through and lightly charred.

• Serve with ice cream and garnish with strawberries.

NOTE: You can prepare these as far as a day ahead for a party. They are an excellent dessert to produce at the end of a complex meal or when there are lots of kids present.

Serves 6
Prep Time: 20 minutes
Cook Time: 15 minutes

SWEET GEORGIA CORNBREAD
WITH GRILLED BANANAS AND BOURBON PECAN CARAMEL SAUCE

9-inch (23 cm) round cake pan or 12-cup muffin pan, greased and floured

CORNBREAD

½ cup	butter, melted and cooled slightly	125 mL
2	large eggs, beaten	2
1	12 oz (341 mL) can cream-style corn	1
1 cup	sour cream	250 mL
1½ cups	all-purpose flour, sifted	375 mL
1½ cups	yellow cornmeal (stone-ground is best)	375 mL
¾ cup	granulated sugar	175 mL
1½ tbsp	baking powder	22 mL
⅛ tsp	salt	0.5 mL

BOURBON PECAN CARAMEL SAUCE

1 cup	granulated sugar	250 mL
1 cup	firmly packed demerara or dark brown sugar	250 mL
⅔ cup	table (18%) cream	150 mL
¼ cup	butter, softened	60 mL
½ cup	bourbon	125 mL
¾ cup	pecans, roughly chopped	175 mL

GRILLED BANANAS

6–12	firm, barely ripe bananas	6–12
1 tsp	ground cinnamon, or to taste	5 mL
pinch	ground nutmeg	pinch
½–1 cup	butter, melted	125–250 mL
1 cup (or more)	whipping (35%) cream, whipped to stiff peaks	250 mL (or more)

Fresh mint leaves (optional)

This is not a dessert for the faint of heart, but the cornbread and sauce can both be prepared well in advance of serving. For variations on a theme, try ice cream instead of (or in addition to) the whipped cream. Add a drizzle of chocolate sauce at the end as a final extravagant flourish. And try other grilled fruit, such as pineapple or pears. Have fun with this one!

• Preheat oven to 375ºF (190ºC).

CORNBREAD: In a bowl, combine the ½ cup (125 mL) butter, eggs, cream-style corn, and sour cream, and mix well.

• In a large bowl, combine flour, cornmeal, the ¾ cup (175 mL) granulated sugar, baking powder, and salt and mix well.

• Add the liquid ingredients to the dry and gently fold them together with a rubber spatula, just enough to blend. There may be a few dry streaks, but don't overmix.

• Bake in the preheated oven for 40 to 45 minutes for the cake pan and 25 to 30 minutes for muffins, or until a wooden skewer inserted into the centre comes out clean.

• If not using right away, allow to cool completely before wrapping well with plastic wrap. Note: At this point, the cornbread can be frozen for up to 3 weeks.

BOURBON PECAN CARAMEL SAUCE: In a heavy saucepan, heat the 1 cup (250 mL) granulated sugar, 1 cup (250 mL) demerara sugar, table cream, and softened butter over medium-high heat. Cook, stirring constantly, to dissolve the sugars and thicken slightly, about 8 to 10 minutes.

• Carefully stir in the bourbon (it may flame for a few seconds), then the nuts. Let stand for at least 10 minutes. Note: The sauce will keep, covered and refrigerated, for 7 to 10 days.

• Preheat grill to medium (350ºF/175ºC) and brush with oil.

GRILLED BANANAS: Whisk the cinnamon and nutmeg into the ½ cup (250 mL) melted butter with a fork.

• Leaving the peel on the bananas, slice in half lengthwise and brush the cut side with the cinnamon butter. Grill, cut side down first, on preheated grill until lightly browned, about 2 minutes. Turn and grill until bananas begin to pull away from peel, about 3 to 4 minutes. Do not overgrill and turn the bananas to mush.

Serves 6 to 12
Prep Time: 45 minutes
Bake time: 45 minutes
Cook Time: 5 minutes

• Split a piece of the corn bread or a muffin in half horizontally. Set the bottom on a plate. Lay some banana slices across the bread and drizzle with the Bourbon Pecan Caramel Sauce. Top with a dollop of whipped cream and set on the top piece of bread at an angle. Top with another banana slice and drizzle with more sauce. Finish with a little more whipped cream and a mint leaf, if desired.

ACKNOWLEDGEMENTS

The Schroeter Family: Ingrid, Wolfgang, Chris, and Stephen, thank you for all your support and encouragement over the past years. Your grills are the best; they make my food sing.

Napoleon Appliance Corporation: Thank you to all those involved at Napoleon in creating the best grills in the world. Your support, talent, and dedication to Napoleon is greatly appreciated.

David Coulson: Thanks for your support over the years. You are a grilling inspiration.

Greg Cosway: My manager — Greg, thanks for all your support over the past year. You truly have put me on the right track and I now know the light at the end of the tunnel is not a train. Pure excitement ahead, my friend; thank you.

Les Murray: My business manager — Les, thanks for your support and direction in helping me find the drive to move things forward. Especially with getting me on the path to healthy living. Cheers to our business.

Key Porter Books: Jordan and the gang at Key Porter — thank you for your support. I know this was not an easy book to put together but it truly is delicious. Your belief in Ted Reader is awesome. Thanks.

Mike McColl: Mike, thank you for all your hard work on this cook book. Your photos are edible. Congratulations on capturing my food. You have been a great asset to my business, not only as my chef but also as my friend. Good luck with your new photographic endeavours.

Wendy Baskerville: Wendy, thank you for taking my ideas and helping me put this book together. You are awesome! It is a pleasure working with you.

Joanne Lusted: Jo Jo, thank you for all your hard work getting this book completed. Muchas gracias, senorita.

Trevor T-Bone Jewer: Hey T-Bone, thanks for all your hard work on getting this book completed. Muchas gracias, amigo.

My wife Pamela: Pamela, my love, thank you for all your support in my career. Your are my rock. You have stood by me through it all. From over 88 grills in the yard to the complete invasion and culinary chaos in your life. Thank you for keeping me motivated, encouraged, and loved. You are my inspiration!

— CHEF TED READER

We couldn't have brought this wonderful cookbook together without the dedication, support, and countless long hours of some of the best people in the industry — our friend Chef Ted Reader and his staff of grilling gurus, Joanne Lusted and Mike McColl (Mike is also the photographer making these mouthwatering dishes come alive). Thanks, too, to Martin Gould and Michael Mouland from Key Porter Books who kept us on track and lent support with their years of experience. Last but not least, we would like to thank all the associates at Napoleon Appliance Corporation who make everything and anything possible.

— INGRID AND WOLFGANG SCHROETER

CREDITS

Chef Ted Reader: Author, recipe development, writing, editing, food styling, prop styling, and BBQ guru

Pamela Jacobsen: Director of BBQ Operations, Ted Reader Inc.

Mike McColl: Photographer

Wendy Baskerville: Recipe development, writing, and editing

Joanne Lusted: Chef/food stylist

Trevor T-Bone Jewer: Chef/food stylist

Greg Cosway: Manager

Les Murray: Business manager

Ralph James: Agent

Blair Holder: Legal council